ZIG-ZAG

BOY

ZIG-ZAG

BOY

A Memoir of Madness and

Motherhood

TANYA FRANK

W. W. NORTON & COMPANY
Celebrating a Century of Independent Publishing

Zig-Zag Boy is a work of nonfiction. Dialogue has been reconstructed to the best of the author's ability. Some names of individuals have been changed, along with potentially identifying characteristics. The approaches, techniques, and remedies referred to or discussed in this book reflect the author's experiences and/or opinions only, are not intended as recommendations, and should not be construed to substitute for medical, therapeutic, or other professional advice.

For information about permission to reproduce selections from this book, write to Permissions, W. W. Norton & Company, Inc., 500 Fifth Avenue, New York, NY 10110

For information about special discounts for bulk purchases, please contact W. W. Norton Special Sales at specialsales@wwnorton.com or 800-233-4830

Manufacturing by LSC Harrisonburg
Production manager: Louise Mattarelliano

ISBN 978-0-393-53188-6

W. W. Norton & Company, Inc., 500 Fifth Avenue, New York, N.Y. 10110
www.wwnorton.com

W. W. Norton & Company Ltd., 15 Carlisle Street, London W1D 3BS

1 2 3 4 5 6 7 8 9 0

For Zach and the elephant seals

"Insanity—a perfectly rational adjustment to an insane world."

—RD LAING

CONTENTS

AUTHOR'S NOTE

Dear reader,

Zig-Zag Boy is a love story, an urgent tale of a fierce battle a mother wages for her child. I worry about telling such a personal story, one that isn't just my own, but I hope that sharing it will help others to feel less alone, to give those of us who contend with psychosis a collective voice. Families like ours live on the edge, in a no-man's-land, our voices often stifled or ignored by bureaucracy and archaic laws. Despite being the closest witness to Zach's suffering, I came to realize that I was often unable to advocate for him, to break through the barriers created by current mental health systems.

Psychosis is often thought to be genetic, or a symptom of brain chemistry gone awry, yet no disease markers show up in brain scans or blood tests. It may well be caused or triggered by the interplay of various factors we are just beginning to understand, from epigenetics to trauma to culture and environment.

For many years I despised Los Angeles, because that was where Zach's psychosis first presented, but now I know that LA didn't cause this experience any more than I did. Psychosis is more complex than this.

I hope that the simple idea of being with someone and not doing to them, of asking what has happened and not what is wrong, will resonate and proliferate. I firmly believe in the privilege of supporting each other in this way and will continue to advocate for such a basic philosophy, which will conserve money as well as lives and help to promote a more compassionate world.

Tanya Frank
February 2023

ZIG-ZAG

BOY

BIRTHING SEASON

WINTER 2017

I walk out to South Point. It is wild and desolate; the air smells of molted seal fur and guano. I take my binoculars so I can see her more clearly—the first elephant-seal mother to haul off. She is lumbering and clumsy as she heaves her body over the dunes and past the willow.

Early winter is birthing season at Año Nuevo, the elephant-seal sanctuary in Northern California where I am training to be a docent. My fellow volunteers are eating lunch in the barn. I am alone out here. Walking helps. I make new footprints in the sand, my skin tingling in the salty air. I clench my fists and release them.

Out on Cove Beach, the surfers in their black wetsuits carve up the face of a wave. My boy used to surf, raising his limber body onto a shortboard. That was when he trusted the water and its purity. I didn't suspect that anything could get in the way of his dreams.

The mother seal dives into the water when the beta males aren't looking. She knows that if she is caught they will try to mate with her, just in case she hasn't been impregnated by the alpha. It doesn't matter that she is spent and famished.

Somehow, she isn't spotted. Her skin shimmers like silver foil as she dips into the surf. She heads out into the deeper, darker water where she moves more easily and only has herself to think about. She doesn't look back at her pup, who lifts up his head and chest from the beach as he searches for her. This is the first time she has left her baby's side since his birth. She has given him all of herself, even when the tides were wild and threatening, when the huge elephant-seal bulls rose around her, roaring and fighting violently for the alpha position, when she was empty from birthing and had lost one-third of her body weight from lactating and fasting.

Now something tells her it is time to leave him, to ignore her pup's cries that carry on the breeze. He continues to call the way he has done for the last month, the sound that had always worked to keep her close and protective of him. But she is far away now, hungry for fish and squid, deep-diving, alone. Her blubbery pup is still too fat to swim, and his buoyancy would attract the sharks. He must slim down and learn when to take the plunge himself. I stare at him, stranded, rejected.

The pups have a fifty percent chance of surviving their maiden voyage, and even if this pup one day makes it back to Año Nuevo, to the very same breeding ground where he was conceived and born, there is no scientific evidence to suggest that he and his mother will ever reunite. The mother will forget the scent of her pup, his cry and the bond they forged during their early days together; she will mate again, give birth and propagate. She is all instinct.

As I stand on the bluff I think about Zach, my youngest son, lying at home, curled up inside his sleeping bag, hands over his ears to shut out the voices only he hears.

My eyes prick with tears behind my sunglasses, and then I am crying more freely, fiercely, and it hurts my throat. I want to climb down to the beach and pick up the seal pup, to feed him myself, but the laws of nature govern here at the reserve. There can be no human intervention.

I leave South Point and make my way back under the low sky. The marine haze is still heavy on the northern side of the reserve.

The other docents gather and take their seats in the old horse barn for the afternoon session. We are going to watch video footage of great white sharks, filmed by researchers at the University of California. I keep my sunglasses on and stand by the door, trying not to panic about the fact that there is no Wi-Fi or cell service here on this remote part of the California coast. I wonder if my son has woken up yet, frantic to reach me, if he will remember to call his older brother instead. I wonder if it is helping at all, me being here, trying to distract myself, trying to become a woman who isn't solely consumed by looking after her son, trying to put him together again.

The shark expert starts his commentary about shark feeding habits, their evolution. It is hard to concentrate, the lecture sounds muffled and the room is airless. I hear something about the bad reputation that great whites have, how it is our responsibility to explain to park visitors why they don't deserve to be feared and hated. It is important to him; I can feel it in the urgency of his delivery and the quiver of his Adam's apple. I recognize that desperation to set the record straight.

1

THE BREAK

Autumn 2009

"This is how they're monitoring us," he whispers, his face stricken, his breath sour. "We have to cut some stuff out, change the receiver. I can do it."

"Who?" I ask. "Who is monitoring us? And why?"

He puts a finger to his lips to quiet me and begins rifling through the toolkit, although he doesn't seem quite sure what he is looking for.

"What's going on?" I whisper.

And this is how it begins, in the laundry room in the late hours, when I find Zach, my nineteen-year-old son, tracing the wires of our defunct telephone circuit board.

He has never rerouted wires in his life, and besides, we suspended our landline service half a decade ago.

I stare at him, his slim body tense, the muscles of his neck straining, fists pumped as if ready to swing at the punching bag that hangs in the basement. His pupils are big. He navigates the familiar space awkwardly, like an intruder, knocking against my mud-splattered bike that leans against the wall. I don't recognize him: his expression, his movements, his demeanor.

"Did you take drugs?" I ask. He shakes his head.

I shiver in this forgotten room. Its concrete floor numbs my bare feet. I'm a Londoner by birth with a tolerance for damp, so I know it's not the cold that has me shaking. I am scared of what is happening to my child.

My partner Nance is in San Francisco for work. My eldest son Dale is in Santa Barbara for college, and we—my younger boy and I—are in Los Angeles, a metropolis of over twelve million people.

Outside it is autumn, the season of turning inward, of gray skies and dormant leaves.

"Sit down," Zach implores. He slides to the floor and props his strong back against the washing machine. I join him, moving a mound of laundry out of the way.

He is taller than me at 5 feet 9 inches, with thick chestnut hair and gold-flecked eyes like mine. His face, forearms and calves—the parts his wetsuit doesn't cover—are still tanned from a long, late summer. He is wearing a nylon t-shirt and football shorts. At close proximity he smells of Axe deodorant spray and garlic.

He had stayed over last night, rather than returning to his shared apartment in Westwood. I'd made him spaghetti with marinara sauce, prepared the way he likes it, with grated Parmesan. He ate every bit (which always pleases the Yiddish mama in me), then retired early to what used to be his room, to work on a mid-term paper for his history degree at UCLA. He was a little tired and withdrawn—which I had put down to the pressures of his studies, or girlfriend troubles—but other than that he appeared fine.

Fine. The very notion seems absurd now, as we sit side by side with his mouth against my ear.

"I'm scared the bad people will hear me talking to you."

A strangled laugh rises in my throat, in part because his hot breath tickles, but mostly because it is my default reaction when I'm nervous. I don't know what to say, what to do. There is no protocol for this new territory. I feel sweat break out on my palms and the back of my neck. When he lunges forward to grab his rucksack, I'm startled.

I watch him take his notebook and a marker pen from his bag. As he zips the compartment back up I see the tip of our large, serrated kitchen knife, the one that went missing last night. Adrenaline courses through my body. My son would never hurt me. I know he wouldn't. It's Zach, for God's sake. My gentle, soft-spoken boy with an easy smile.

I sit on the floor in silence, my breathing shallow. He focuses intently on the task he has assigned himself. His wavy hair falls around his face as he leans forward to write:

> *Mike and Josh are not really my friends.*
> *They are members of the Russian Mafia out to harm me.*
> *UCLA is a network set up to spy on me.*
> *Our computers and cell phones are bugged.*

Everything I know about how to parent is tested in this moment. I place my hand on his forehead, which is warm but not overly so. "Stay here," I instruct him firmly, as if he is a dog that might dash out the door. I grab the thermometer from the bathroom and place it under his tongue, praying that he has a fever-induced delirium that will pass with a dose of aspirin, but it reads 98.6. Normal. Dread swells in my chest.

"Come on, Zigs," I encourage, helping him up. "I think you're tired out."

I guide him back to bed with my hand on his shoulder, the way I used to do when he was little. His old room, in the basement of our three-story house that clings to the Old Hollywood hillside, is a far cry from the council flat in East London where we used to live. It has always been a surreal pleasure to live here, but suddenly the steps are too many, the house too big, daybreak and Nance too far away.

I tuck him in, hoping he will go to sleep and wake up his old self—with the kind eyes and strong Jewish nose like mine, the boy who still belly-laughs his way through old *Simpsons* episodes, who loves to surf overhead waves at Malibu Beach, and can play anything on the piano by ear. The son I am so proud of.

My hope is futile. He can't rest. Los Angeles has insomnia too; it is perma-young and edgy, a city on steroids. Police sirens drift up from the flatlands and the coyotes howl in response. Zach gets up and peeks out from under the blinds at the window. In the distance, news helicopters whirr above the Hollywood Walk of Fame for the debut of *Avatar*.

"See, I told you," he whispers, so quietly that I have to strain to make out the words. "I'm under surveillance. They're reading my mind. They're coming for me."

There is a hitch of pure terror in his voice that I haven't heard since he was a child, when, after catching a few scenes of *Frankenstein* on television, he had had terrible nightmares. They seemed to stretch on for weeks, and I would wake up with him next to me in my bed. It is as if we have traveled back in time. His fear is all-consuming. He won't let me leave his side.

It is only when our Bedlington terrier, Belle, settles at our feet and Zach reaches out to touch her that I let out my breath. It is a good sign, finally—a boy and his dog. He had begged for her when he was eleven, paying her adoption fee from the sale of his Pokémon cards and never looking back. He was an earnest kid with Harry Potter glasses—and smart too, a chess whizz, when the rest of us didn't even know the rules. In my mind's eye I can still see the look on his face, that shy delight when he came home with the trophy.

I leave him with Belle while Suki, our other dog, follows me to the toilet. I pee and call Nance. Her voicemail kicks in. "Honey, it's me. I need to talk to you. It's urgent. There's something wrong with Zach."

Zach knocks on the toilet door and my heart jolts. I flush the chain and try to squeeze the fear from my chest, straighten my mouth, relax my jaw where I hold the bulk of my tension. I wonder how much he heard. I don't want to do anything to worsen his distrust, to fuel any fear that we will join ranks, his two mothers, against him.

"Can you stay with me?" he asks.

"Sure," I say. I follow him, holding my phone with a tense grip, checking the battery level surreptitiously and switching it to vibrate.

Zach crawls under his blankets and pulls them up over his face. I sit next to him, resting my hand on his shoulder, trying to soothe us both.

I stay until the sun begins to climb above the palm trees and the blue jays chirp as if everything is right with the world. My phone buzzes in my pocket. It's Nance. I move stealthily from the room to talk to her in private. I hear her getting ready for work. Nance is a commercial producer. Her day will be full of studio or location commotion, actors, video crews, camera equipment, and now this. She is not panicky by nature, and her steadfast, unruffled tone calms me.

"Maybe give it a bit longer," she says. "He might just be having a bad trip."

"But he's been here the whole time," I say, as if bad trips only happen at raves and in the company of one's peers.

"Well, if he doesn't seem better by tonight," Nance says, "then perhaps you should take him to the hospital, just to let them assess him."

I hang up. My stomach is roiling. The day slows as I focus intently on Zach. He doesn't eat breakfast, or lunch, or dinner. He looks out of the basement windows onto the cul-de-sac as if he is expecting someone. He stares at himself in the mirror with a curiosity that is novel and perplexed. I ask him again if he has taken drugs, if he has a headache, if he fell in the night, but he says no, and I believe him.

As the night closes in, I think about what Nance said. I feign conviction and tell Zach we need to go to the emergency room. He looks at me with wide eyes, scared and doubting, as if I've announced an imminent betrayal. I feel myself recoil. I'm his mum. But he nods and swings his legs out of bed. I shuffle him upstairs and into our Volvo, buckling him up in the front seat and activating the child-safety locks. Just in case. As we head west toward the ocean and the Ronald Reagan UCLA Medical Center, his eyes dart from billboards to people on the sidewalk to car license plates. I drive slowly, focusing on my breath.

"What's happening to me?" he says. "What did I do to make me a target like this?" I tell him he must be exhausted, maybe suffering the stress of exams, and that I hope they will give him something to help him sleep. I can't tell whom I'm trying hardest to reassure.

The emergency room is quiet, with just a handful of people dotted around on the vinyl seats. A television screen, the sound off, dances in a corner. We are ushered promptly into a private cubicle, temperature-controlled and sterile, where Zach is asked to don a blue gown and plastic ID bracelet, and to vacate to the bathroom so he can urinate in a specimen cup. Back in the cubicle, a nurse takes his vital signs. Pulse. Temperature. Blood pressure.

"All normal," she confirms.

"That's great, Zigs," I say.

But instead of being directed to another department for further tests, or to the pharmacy to pick up medication, we are asked to wait, which we do. Machines blink and bleep, and staff in pale-blue uniforms and sensible shoes race along the brightly lit corridors. The chaos that exists behind the calm façade of the reception is unsettling. It is everything that we don't want to see at such a fretful time: the skid of carts on linoleum, scurrying bodies, the clatter of clipboards, bright lights and hurried, half-caught conversations.

A nurse bustles in to ask about Zach's physical health, what medications he takes, whether he is allergic to anything. I think she asks him if he has eaten and drunk and slept, but I am distracted by a piece of blue tape on her nose that covers her piercing, and a band-aid on her arm, a tattoo leaking out around the edges.

She takes notes, flares her nostrils, and the tape crinkles. Then she leaves.

Zach wants to leave too. He has changed his mind. He shuts his eyes and cocks his head to one side, and I can tell he hears something I can't, senses danger heading toward us that I do not comprehend. I am aching for him to play by the rules, to appear good and sane enough to be sent home. I want to feel safe and comforted by the fact that we are in a hospital, a place with doctors and nurses. My mum brought me up to think that doctors were gods and nurses were angels, that they miraculously cured people. As children, my siblings and I were taken to the GP at the first sign of a sniffle or cough. I was given so much tetracycline for tonsilitis that it caused staining to my adult teeth when they came through, but mum—up until her last breath at just sixty-one—still trusted medical professionals. I want to believe she was right to have faith in them. Perhaps I can instill confidence in Zach this way too. We can find out what we need from the doctor and then get back on the road, homeward bound, where we belong.

I peek out at the other patients. Some of them are moaning, bandaged and bloodstained. I try to pass off my nagging doubt, the sense of wanting to flee the scene, my boy and me. Perhaps we could start over: more sleep, more bolognaise, more quiet time with the curtains drawn and Belle snuggled between us on the bed, the thing that soothes us, or at least used to, before today.

I look up to notice that we have been assigned a security guard, who is posted outside the room. Protocol, I tell myself.

After another round of questions and more monitoring of Zach's temperature and blood pressure, a female psychiatrist with kind brown eyes and a daisy-print dress asks to talk to Zach alone, then to me privately, and finally to both of us together. I recount the events of the last twenty-four hours, and before I've finished my last sentence, I am signing papers to admit him into the psychiatric ward for a seventy-two-hour hold. I realize how tightly I have been clinging on to the hope that somebody might offer us a concrete medical explanation so we can fix it. So we can fix him.

Zach's eyes flit left and right. He wants to know if his room will have a lock on it; his voice is urgent as he continues to insist that the mob are after him.

"Everything is going to be okay, Zach," I say, trying to wrap my arm around him like I did last night, though reaching him on the gurney is awkward. I notice the strip of pale flesh where his wrist-watch has been removed. His glasses are gone, too, stuffed with his clothes into a clear plastic bag. He suddenly looks sicker than when we arrived. He squints at me as I wave goodbye. I don't know how to leave him. Am I supposed to turn and walk out onto Westwood Plaza? Everything has shifted on its axis, and I can't undo it.

I drive home alone, slipping down the side streets of Holly-wood and up to our hilltop. The city below is an orange shimmer of glass and steel skyscrapers. I park in the carport and stay there, too stunned to move. I cannot shake a vision of my boy being held down and injected with drugs that make him drool and shuffle. This thing has swallowed my son, locking him into, and me out of this city that seems suddenly hostile and foreign.

I make my way into the house and slump onto the bed. I feel something deflate in me, and I'm left with nothing but a few sad, shallow breaths.

2

PSYCHOSIS NOS

The first time I saw elephant seals I was happy. We all were, especially Zach.

It was our first Thanksgiving holiday, and Nance had suggested that we take the long way up to her childhood home in the San Francisco Bay Area to celebrate with her folks. The drive took us along Highway 1 through Big Sur, or "God's country," as it was called by the locals. This long strip of coastline is home to some of the deepest underwater canyons, the richest kelp forests and an abundance of marine mammals.

The farther north we went the more rugged the landscape became, and the boys, unperturbed by the swell, surfed at various spots along the way. We were a couple of miles north of San Simeon when I saw them from the bluffs above Piedras Blancas Beach. At first sight they looked like gray boulders strewn around the sand, perfectly still, big inanimate lumps of granite. But when I looked more carefully through Nance's binoculars that I had strung around my neck, I spied them beneath the willow, under the beating-hot sun—elephant seals. Real live beasts, moving their flippers, digits and fingernails visible as they scratched their bellies and flicked sand over their backs. They were enormous, especially the males, as long as the rented SUV we were traveling in. I wavered between reverence and revulsion as I focused on the scarred, mottled chest-shields of the alpha males.

"Look, look!" I shouted to Nance and Dale and Zach, wanting to share this otherworldly scene of these prehistoric-looking animals. "I thought they were rocks."

Afterward, when we were settled back in the car, warm and close to each other, and in motion, I realized the sheer size and spectacle of what I had just witnessed. Like the enormity of the seals' bodies, it was almost too much to behold. I knew there and then that there was a wild magic about these beasts, and the fact that they could haul out just a few feet from Highway 1.

Like their fellow Californian creatures the scrub-jay, the Channel Island fox and the bald eagle, these gargantuan animals had been hunted to near extinction. Their species had dwindled to a bottleneck. It was a miracle that they had survived and were now at healthy enough numbers that they could be taken off the endangered list and placed on the protected one.

•

Lying in bed in our Hollywood home, I feel cold. I turn over, burrow under the quilt and start to cry at the memory of that day; my infatuation with Nance, with the land, and these animals. Before now, I had assumed, perhaps naively, that we had come through the worst: my mum's passing in 2004, too soon, too painful. The loss of Auntie Betty during that same wretched year.

Since then, a full five years on, we had survived an expensive bureaucratic process to get our green cards. The golden state is now our home. We belong, and have the papers to prove it. And yet, despite our affiliation to America, it is as if we don't fit so neatly anymore.

Until recently, on nights like this when the sky was clear, Zach journeyed with Dale to the Pacific Palisades on the West Side of Los Angeles. Complete with shortboards, wetsuits and all the energy of youth, they went surfing, bracing the wind and the swell of the currents. They wore neon-green glow sticks around their necks so they could watch out for each other after dusk.

Zach has good friends, steadfast ones of seven years whom he has planned to kayak with around the Channel Islands, to motorbike with through the desert. One of them has an RV. Another is building a light aircraft and has access to his father's small sailboat. The plans sound impressive, the kind of once-in-a-lifetime missions born out of privilege and vitality. I wonder what will happen from here on out, whether Zach will still be able to join them and do these things he has been looking forward to.

Everyone loves Zach, and the many strings he has to his bow. Before he left home to live on campus at UCLA he would entertain the hilltop neighbors by reading them pages from his novel-in-progress. This chatty, precocious teen of mine could be found playing with the dogs, or doing his homework so he could get the scores needed to be accepted to a top-tier university. It wasn't just Nance and I who recognized Zach's scholarly talents. He had been admitted into all kinds of clubs and advanced placement programs at high school, as well as Debate Society and Theater Studies. His brother Dale has his own strengths too. He's streetwise, a natural comedian, and a gifted singer–songwriter and guitarist. When Zach decided to pick up the guitar and teach himself how to play, I'd cringed a tad. "I wish he would just leave that one thing in Dale's corner," I'd told Nance.

•

I look at my watch, the big face on the wide, brown leather strap that Nance got for me. I'm keeping track of the next seventy-two hours during which Zach will be kept in the psych ward for observation. In California this is known as a 5150 hold.

I am very much alive, still breathing in and out, but I can't quite fathom what to do with myself. Time stretches into the kind of void I have rarely experienced, aside from when mum died, or my boys were born. I call the hospital, who tell me that Zach is sleeping peacefully, but I'm unconvinced. His phone has been taken away. I have no way of checking in with him directly. I feel distrustful, suspicious. All the things that he has been detained for.

Sleeping peacefully is the kind of language that is reserved for post-surgery patients, people who are in terrible pain. I want to sleep peacefully too, to be knocked out, sedated, but even if I had the means, I know I need to be alert, ready for anything in case he needs me, in case of a bad reaction to the situation. I am the adult. I must be calm and in control.

I rub tiger balm into my neck. It makes my eyes water.

I imagine Zach in a single metal-frame bed. Again, I wonder if they've given him any drugs, and how he is feeling.

I will the hands on my watch to move faster, as if I am Uri Geller. As a little girl, when my first wristwatch—a red Timex—started to slow, mum encouraged me to fetch it from my jewelry box, sit cross-legged in front of the TV and hold it out like a gift to the self-proclaimed psychic. Uri fixed it. He could bend metal too. He called it psychokinesis, and when under hypnosis he claimed that his power was given to him by aliens.

My watch today is quartz, like my old Timex, but it is heavy, and the suede underside of the strap makes my wrist sweat. I look again with much intent, but the hands don't move any quicker; they may have even slowed down. I don't think I believe in Uri Geller anymore. I don't know what I believe in right now.

Nance calls from the airport. She is taking the rest of the week off work and making her way back home.

"I am so grateful," I tell her.

"Of course," she says. "Of course."

I enter the bathroom and fill the tub, more hot than cold, the way mum liked it. I miss her. I miss Zach. Each absence winds around the other, a tight plait of loss and grief that I can't untangle. Inching my body down into the old porcelain bath, my skin reddens in the heat. Free-floating soothes me. I have put on weight in recent months, but the water still lifts and lightens me. I think of the elephant-seal colony at Piedras Blancas, my special place.

I close my eyes in the steam. I hear the waves and the wind, and I see the outlines of the elephant seals that haul out at the beach. These marine mammals float and dive, but they also sink. Instruments have tracked their slow descent to depths of up to five thousand feet in waters darker than night and icy cold. They have adapted to be able to hold their breath for up to two hours and shunt their blood supply from their extremities to their vital organs, entering a state of rest that might be compared to sleep apnea, but they always surface in the end. Despite the risk of predators, they come up to the light in the shallows, to replenish oxygen, to breathe.

•

After seventy-two hours in the psychiatric ward, Zach's assessment is over. He is going to be released. Nance is back, and she drives me to collect him. They cut off his wristband and hand him a clear plastic bag with his medication and discharge notes. As we make our way home, I look back at him to try to see where he splintered. He looks whole to me. There is an earnestness about him that feels familiar. This could be a one-off episode, I think, a temporary thing. I can't tear my eyes away from him, and I make a promise to myself that Zach will get through this, and we'll never have to mention this chapter in history to anyone.

I open the car windows and the breeze hits my cheek, warm and damp as if a storm is brewing.

Back home, I escape to the bedroom and perch on the chair. With a jittering hand I open the envelope containing the discharge notes. Zach's symptoms have been examined and classified as if he were some rare and delicate butterfly, and he has emerged with a diagnosis of Psychosis NOS (Not Otherwise Specified), a vague kind of *darned if I know* label. The evidence is scanty, but it suggests that my boy has had a psychotic break, the term they use when someone detaches from their psyche.

It is almost impossible to form sentences when Nance tries to speak to me, because I am dead tired, and the word *psychosis* sticks in my throat. Zach is exhausted too, and he doesn't want to talk about what he has been through. All he manages to say is that he never wants to go back to the hospital. He doesn't understand how I could have allowed it, his own mother. I tell him not to worry, there is absolutely no way I will let it happen again. "Not over my dead body," I say.

"Do you swear on Nan's ashes?" he asks, because we can't swear on her life anymore.

"I swear on Nan's ashes."

"Nothing crossed?"

"Nope, nothing crossed." I show him my hands and stretch out my fingers.

Crossing makes the promise void. I'm not sure why, it just does.

After dinner, which he sniffs a few times, his lids grow heavy, and he falls asleep on the couch. I sit next to him, relieved he is home, but strangely numb. Ungrounded, unearthed like the outdated two-prong outlets in this house, I might even be dangerous. I push my feet firmly into the hardwood floor. I need to be here, all of me.

Nance tells Zach she loves him before she goes to bed. I could swear she has tears in her eyes. My Nance—the most stoic person I've ever known. She tucks the blanket around his feet. He stirs. I know from the concerned way she looks at me she thinks I should try to get some sleep too. But I have work to do.

I switch on my laptop and look up psychosis. It is described on various websites as losing touch with reality, and may involve seeing things, hearing voices or having delusions. According to the sources, one in a hundred people will experience a psychotic episode in their lifetime.

My body starts to tremble and my teeth chatter as I read how it can be caused by substance abuse, how even before the first episode there may be alterations in the way the person thinks and behaves.

This is called the prodromal period. It can last days, weeks, months, or even years.

What did I miss? I wonder. I know Zach had trouble waking in the mornings during the last year of high school, and that he was moody at times. Nance said it was common. Americans even have a name for it: senioritis. But there was something else. The excessive amount of marijuana. We found it in his car in little plastic bags, in his rucksack in small pots. It smelled stronger than anything I had ever smoked, and it was labeled Purple Kush, Sativa, Indica.

In time I will find out how marijuana with a THC (tetrahydro-cannabinol) level over ten percent is believed to play a role in those who experience psychosis. I will berate myself when I read these claims. Zach's aunt, equally critical, will ask me more than once, when we talk on the phone, "Why didn't you stop him from smoking weed?"

For every theory, though, there is an argument that runs counter to it. Some experts maintain that the marijuana does not cause the extreme state, but is instead used to numb the pain that comes with it. I read more interpretations. Lack of sleep, brain tumors or cysts, chromosomal disorders, some types of epilepsy and genetics are all said to play a role.

Some psychosis is short-lived, described by the medical profession as a brief psychotic disorder which occurs during times of extreme stress or trauma. People in this category will generally come out of the altered state in a few days to a few weeks, depending on the source of stress.

Sitting as we are, together on the couch, I stare at my son. His chiseled cheekbones, long eyelashes and tanned complexion. He is so handsome. I pray that he will be back to himself in no time, that this is a momentary blip. I lean across him and brush his hair from his face. How can anyone diagnose someone after asking a few questions and watching their behavior for three short days? It's bullshit, I tell myself. But still, as I read about the potential complications and prognosis, something flutters in my sternum like a trapped hummingbird. I cannot stop reading, the shock and numbness of just an hour ago giving way to fear as I learn that if left without medical treatment, people experiencing psychosis struggle to take good care of themselves.

When my neck is stiff and my shoulders ache from hunching over the computer I join Nance, but I cannot sleep. The mating call of the male crickets vibrates from the canyon. Normally soothing, it is deafening tonight.

I am not the only restless soul in the house. Zach has woken up. I hear the pull and push of the refrigerator door in the basement kitchen. I imagine him feeding through the dark hours like a fruit bat, even though he has had supper. I want to go downstairs, nudge his arm, call him Drac, try to make him laugh like I used to with our family repertoire of silly names. But I do not move. My body is heavy. Zach's diagnosis, as tenuous as it is, is too much for my fatigued brain to take in. As the night cools, the crickets stop rubbing their leathery wings together. It quietens.

The rest of the night stretches out, long and fitful, and when the light breaks outside I realize that Nance is already awake and upstairs making tea. Staying put, I read the discharge instructions from the psychiatric hospital again and again, and question how scanty they are. Aside from notes about how to take his medication, and a follow-up appointment at the mental health clinic in Hollywood that is not for another week, there are no clear guidelines.

I think about the day ahead, the weeks ahead. I feel something settle like liquid steel in my stomach; I can feel my body physically bracing itself for impact.

3

FORMIDABLE

When I try to fill his prescription at the pharmacy for Abilify—a drug that is named an antipsychotic, but some say is really a tranquilizer—the pharmacist tells me it will cost twelve hundred dollars, as our health insurance does not cover it. Zach is nonchalant, but I am shocked. I call the hospital and the staff tell me they are not allowed to discuss Zach's care with me, unless he gives written permission, because he is over eighteen. I want to cry, right there in the middle of Rite Aid pharmacy. The pharmacist takes pity on us and suggests that we visit a free clinic with a walk-in service, where we can be signed up to a program that will provide us with free psychiatric drugs.

The waiting room at this free clinic on Hollywood Boulevard is windowless. There are showers and miniature bars of soap for the homeless. It smells musty. We wait, one, two, three hours.

"I'm not staying," Zach says, and he ups and leaves, without the drugs.

Back home, a sense of utter helplessness hits me. Now I am in familiar surroundings I give in to the urge to weep. Nance closes our bedroom door and I cry into my pillow so that Zach doesn't hear me. My head pounds and there is pressure behind my eyes. I take two Tylenol extra-strength tablets and begin a barrage of phone calls to the health-insurance company, the college campus health center and the pharmacy.

They talk in a foreign language, using terms like co-pays, deductibles, pre-existing conditions, and the difference between generic and named brands of psychiatric drugs. I catch sight of my bloodshot eyes and a harried expression in the bathroom mirror. Finally, it is agreed I can pick up the drugs from the pharmacy, if I have a copy of Zach's ID, and that there will be a five-dollar co-pay. I still don't understand the initial miscalculation, but I say thank you as if I do. The cost has just come down by 1,195 dollars.

I splash my face with cold water and prepare to leave the house—again.

I walk past Zach's room. His door is shut, and I hear music blaring from inside. How normal this moment appears—my teenage son, holed up behind a locked door with his tunes at full volume. For a beat I wonder if I am doing the right thing. It is a fleeting thought before I grab my purse and leave the house.

The pharmacist explains that the prescribed low starting dose of psychiatric drugs is apparently the norm. There are instructions to increase slowly to avoid side effects. So it surprises me when I awake the next day to find Zach perched on the edge of the couch with his knees bouncing up and down—his hands on them trying to still his movements. His eyes twitch and his tongue flicks in and out like the bearded dragon he kept as a boy. He walks around the house for no reason other than that his mind and body won't let him be still.

By mid-morning he is ravenous. He builds himself a triple-decker sandwich, slathering the bread with an odd combination of fillings—peanut butter, cheese and salsa. He shuffles between the fridge and the counter more times than seems necessary. His hands shake as he piles a mountain of potato chips on the side of his plate.

He lands back down hard on the couch, his legs shaking, choppy and rough.

"I feel like there's something inside of me, something trying to get out," he says between lip-smacking bites. His distress makes my stomach lurch.

I place my feet flat on the floor and brace myself, to try and quell the effects of his jittery legs.

I call the hospital. This time I am allowed to speak to someone, a nurse. She tells me to call the mental health clinic where we have our pending appointment, because now that Zach has been discharged the psychiatric ward is no longer responsible for his care. I finally get through to an intake coordinator at the clinic. I am unable to speak to the psychiatrist. I do have Zach's permission now, but that does not help as the psychiatrist is currently with a patient. I feel dizzy from being passed around, from Zach's restlessness, from this fast, furious ride we are on.

The intake coordinator calls me back after speaking to the psychiatrist. It has a name, the restless syndrome.

"Akathi—what? Can you spell it for me?" I ask.

The line is full of static, and though I press the receiver to my ear, his voice is thick and fuzzy. It takes three attempts to decipher what he says. I stare at the word in my diary. Akathisia. I have dotted the *i*s with so much pressure that they break through the page.

"What on earth can we do?" I ask. "He can't live like this. It's as if he has St. Vitus dance."

"It's counteracted by Benztropine. The doctor will fax a prescription through to the local pharmacy."

"So basically, he needs to take a second prescribed drug to counteract the side effects of the first one?"

"It might be helpful."

"Thank you," I say.

I want to say fuck you, not thank you. I don't feel grateful for Zach's diagnosis, for the drugs that cause such debilitating side effects, for a label that carries a stigma so unthinkable.

Zach's eyes scan his empty plate. "I'm still hungry," he says, "but I also feel sick." He returns to the kitchen. I hear him rummaging through the food cupboards, as if he might stifle the thing inside of him with another sandwich, and I feel tears well up in me again, tears I don't know how to explain to him without exacerbating his distress.

When we arrive at the pharmacy for the third time in two days, Zach is convinced that people are following us. Worse still, he believes they intend to harm us. He sneaks up and down the cold and flu aisle looking for them; the coarse, dark hairs on his legs spill over his socks. I traipse after him and we reach the counter together. I fake a calm voice to ask for the prescription.

"Let's sit here," I say, pointing to a row of plastic chairs either side of the blood-pressure machine and the weighing scales. We wait for the prescribed drugs, and I feel a bone-deep fatigue descend upon me.

At home, Zach joins me in the kitchen where I measure out his Benztropine to counteract the Abilify. I will learn that all this over-prescribing has a name, too: polypharmacy. Zach swears under his breath, and I feel his irritability course through my veins like it's contagious. His restlessness finally ceases, but it is replaced with another side effect called akinesia—a noticeable decreased spontaneity. It is as if his brain has suffered such exhaustion that he is too tired to wake up.

As if this isn't enough, there is another thing that seems to plague my boy. Voices. Even when he is sedated and supine and closes his eyes to try to sleep. He hears his cousin and his friends from UCLA, they are mean and belittling. He asks me to focus intently to try to hear them too, convinced they are coming from the houses down on the cul-de-sac or the large triplex on Sycamore Avenue. "I think those properties are too far away, Zach," I tell him. "And why would Braedon be there, or your friends from UCLA?" I pull back the curtain to prove that nobody is outside. I want to be gentle, but I am alarmed. This is a new thing that correlates with the hospitalization and starting the drugs.

"Maybe put your fingers in your ears, and see if you can still hear anything?" I suggest. Zach plugs his ears and shakes his head and looks at me with such puzzlement. I feel my fists clench, but there isn't anyone I can hit out at for the bullying words. They are coming from Zach. He is enemy as well as victim. He is hurting himself and it feels torturous to watch.

Later that night, I tumble into a vortex of cybergroups and chat rooms where I sneak around like a stalker, hungry to learn from peers and family members of those with psychosis. I read and write until the first light steals through the wrought-iron bars of our Juliet balcony. My eyes sting, and my body feels empty from insomnia.

Dale comes home for a few days. There are moments when Zach is very much his old self, shimmying across the wood floor, cupping his crotch, doing Michael Jackson's moonwalk. He does the robot too, and makes his tummy wobble. We laugh then, almost too hard, for too long.

When Dale and I are alone, I dare to ask him the things I've been too scared to ask myself. "What do you know? What do you remember? Was I a bad mother?"

He is not forthcoming. He doesn't want to hurt my feelings. He sees how crumpled my face looks. Soon enough, new silver hairs will slide out of my bandana. They say that shock can turn your hair gray, but I thought it was a myth. Dale looks different too. He is paler and more cautious. I consider the irony of Dale training to be an emergency medical technician, and how he is now in the throes of an emergency that is off the clock, one that he hasn't been prepared for. None of us have.

On the fourteenth day after Zach's release from the hospital, Nance says, "Tan, come on, let's get out for a bit. Dale is here to watch Zach." She leashes Belle and Suki and manages to guide me back to Runyon Canyon Park, 160 acres of hiking trails above the city, our daily place of refuge in times past. This protected wilderness was one of the first spots that Nance showed us when we landed in California. The rugged terrain has ruins of a pool house that, rumor has it, was owned by Errol Flynn. From high above the remains of the estate, a bench overlooks a vertigo-inducing view of the entire city.

Erosion has clawed away the dusty soil atop the ridge, raising the seat high from the ground. The memory of hoisting twelve-year-old Zach up onto the warm, wooden slats is so clear to me, the gritty sole of his boot as he placed it in my open palms so I could give him a leg up. Nance and I either side of him, snapping pictures of us giggling and squinting in the sun. Selfies before they were called selfies.

Nance had pointed out Sunset Strip in the far distance, and the road that led up to our house. This spot where we sat, thighs touching, feet floating in the air, was called Inspiration Point. Aptly so, I thought.

Rock stars and actors use Runyon Canyon Park like their own backyard. KD Lang, Sheryl Crow, Queen Latifah, Ellen DeGeneres. We saw each one of them on different occasions. Runyon, or simply "The Canyon," as we locals named it, was a dog-owner's paradise. Our happy place, where we sweated and chatted and breathed deeply. But that was then, back when the twinkling grid of LA and the steep ridges offered a sense of promise.

•

The Canyon feels more beautiful than ever today, but tragically so, with its pink-gray twilight and rising moon. Back in 1867, it was called No Man's Canyon, and was used as a seasonal home by the nomadic Gabrielino Tongva tribe, before they were forcibly exiled.

"I'm glad we came," Nance says. We stand together at the start of the trail, her arms stretched tight around me, one hand rubbing my back. The daylight is slipping away, and so are our words. There is so little left to say that makes sense. Our son is lost, off-kilter, unwell, that much we know, but I don't want to use the P-word about him. It makes me feel especially queasy today.

Nance is less scared. She is a steady anchor, stronger than me, her body straight up and down, and sinewy. She runs faster, hikes harder, without excess weight to carry. I used to feel this surge of frustration when people asked which of us had birthed the boys. It seemed intrusive, their implicit judgment as they sized up our bodies, eyes lingering on my wide hips, large breasts. Nance never seemed offended. "Tan is their biological mum," she would tell them, and her amiable nature soon had me nodding along, happy to be in a partnership regardless of who had been the one to get impregnated.

Zach's experience alters everything, though, and his diagnosis, which now has a momentum all of its own, is big enough to change my mind. It does matter that I gave birth. Every cell in my body recalls that Zach once lived inside me, that I carried him on my hip, that I moved him across the world at the age of twelve, that I parented him for ten whole years alone after his father and I separated. Nance can sleep at night; she can eat, work and remain unfettered. For this I am grateful, for this I am jealous, for this I am sometimes resentful.

"Look!" she says, pointing at a V-shaped flock of geese flying west toward the ocean, the leader flapping furiously, fighting the currents so the others can glide in its wake. It is still warm from the heat of the day—golden hour, the time just before sunset when the light is soft and full of magic.

"I wish Zach could be here with us," I say, remembering again how much he liked to trek up this mighty hill. This view of the gray-green Santa Monica Mountains shrouded in the LA haze, a world away from the dank London we left behind.

A large, brown Labrador bounds by and sniffs at Belle. I imagine my boy, his sociable, animal-loving self, reaching out to pet the chocolate-colored beast. As a young boy, Zach used to talk to dogs, whispering in their ears, professing they talked back to him. It was the cutest thing to witness, our modern-day Doctor Dolittle.

He will continue to hear animals speak, mostly birds. They will coo in loving admiration of his romance with his girlfriend at college, then they will turn mean and begin taunting him, squawking about how he should take to the streets and become homeless. It won't be endearing anymore. It will be classed as a symptom, an auditory hallucination.

Suki distracts me momentarily, her blonde fur fluttering in the breeze. Belle, although less elegant than her counterpart, is more precious to Zach. Her coat is more wiry than smooth, more wool than fur, aside from a soft patch of white on her chest. As a small boy, Zach used to go to sleep stroking that part of her. He said it smelled of candy, gave him the power to turn off his light and sleep through the night.

The Labrador has gone. The image of Zach with Belle dissolves too. I think of my boy in the here and now, back at the house, too scared to leave his room.

"Maybe we should go back home?" I suggest, feeling exposed and fragile in the darkening canyon.

"Dale is with him," Nance reminds me, "and besides, we only just got here."

Above us on the upper ridge of the park, the scrub oaks and syca- mores cling to the wet, rocky outcrop. The drought-resistant yarrow and Spanish broom cover the lower slope, replenished from El Niño, having made it through another brutal summer. I look at Nance's furrowed forehead and wonder if we can survive here like these Cali- fornian natives.

As she leads the way up the narrow trail, I trudge behind her like a mule with a heavy load. Despite it being almost dusk, the canyon is teeming with people, far too many for my liking. Formidable, our nickname for Runyon's highest peak, used to offer us solace, but today it towers above us, casting a shadow at our feet.

We finally reach the summit and Nance reels me in close again. Feeling her arms around me, I start to cry. It feels to me like a part of Zach has died and I am mourning him.

"You never signed up for this," I tell her between sobs.

"We're in this together," she says firmly. "We're family." She unravels me, urges me along the short plateau before the trail descends. Taking my hand and her own, she tucks them both into the pocket of her jacket where they fit snugly against the seam.

We have been together for seven years now and lived together for five. Before Nance moved in with us she rented a cabin a few doors down from our big house on the hill. Her enchanting little home was said to have been built for one of the Marx brothers. It was her square-faced, wire-haired fox terrier, Oscar, who introduced us to each other, sticking his snout through the railings of my aunt's garden, searching for food. I noticed her dimpled smile, Celtic green eyes and short, brown hair that waved around her neck. Her eyes and dimpled cheeks remain the same, but her hair has grown long, and Oscar is no more.

"If there's anything I can do," she offered all those summers ago, having heard about our situation and my aunt's decline. It was the first time I had set eyes on her, and as brief as our encounter was, there was something about her that made me suppose she was gay. It was her generosity, though, that gesture to help that stayed with me after our meeting, deepening my attraction to her.

"Who is she?" I had asked my aunt, after Nance had wrestled Oscar away and made her way back down the hill. "The pretty neighbor with the funny dog?" Auntie didn't know, or she had forgotten, but she smiled at my rosy cheeks and the swell of excitement growing in me.

They say that you fall in love when you least expect it. Despite such untimeliness, or maybe precisely because of it, I was completely smitten with this gal down the street. Nance confessed that she had never wanted children, preferring dogs and cats instead, yet when I watched her donning a wetsuit so she could catch waves with the boys, fixing sloppy joes for their supper, herding them into her sporty black Saab to take them skateboarding or listening to them as they sang off-key or pressed the wrong chords on guitar, I knew she was the one. Of all my girlfriends, she was the most singularly attentive to Dale and Zach. She made me want a partner again, a co-parent. Family.

There was no way I could return to the world I had left behind. I would find a way to make us all happy. That was what mothers did.

It was a job well done—or so I thought—this forging of a deep relationship of mutual trust over the years. But it isn't enough to hold me in that moment. Suddenly, Nance's cute looks and her loyalty cease to matter to me and I wish I hadn't met her. I feel like I would rather be alone, isolated and backed into Griefville, the town I have started to dwell in. I know exactly where I stand there on the map of emotions, with no one else to worry about or feel beholden to.

•

As we reach the Formosa gate to exit Runyon Canyon, Nance suggests that we might want to consider getting a second opinion, a private doctor to re-evaluate Zach's distressing experiences, and that she can dip into her savings to pay for it. I nod and try not to cry again. Her hand grips mine tightly.

"You can look online at the medical reviews," she says, as if we are in the market for a new washing machine rather than a good psychiatrist. I clutch at the notion that it might be that simple—that you get what you pay for. We just need to find an expert in the field who can tell us what to do, how to live, how to make Zach better, give him a diagnosis that isn't as laden with fear and loathing. We need reassurance that this seeming break from consensual reality is just a one-off episode and not a true psychotic disorder, whatever that means.

Nance squeezes my shoulder, and we smile at one another. It feels good. The air is soft between my fingers, light as organza, scented with eucalyptus. I breathe deeply. I am present. I am back. I need her. I want her. I can't do this alone.

As we make our way home, I peer down over the shelf of granite into the flatlands. I love the night-time view from up here. Homes become plankton on a moonlit sea, and roads weave out like luminescent tentacles. This city is built to order on a geographical axis, with nothing left to chance. It is why we came here, to start again. It is why so many people come here. It is why it is called the New World. The City of Angels.

Back inside the house, I try to hold on to my hope, but the fluorescent lights in the kitchen give me a headache. Nance pours herself a beer with what seems like more readiness than usual. I can't blame her. If only I liked the taste, I would join her in this evening ritual, and embrace the release that alcohol might bring.

I leave Dale and Nance in their separate galaxies, and slowly make my way down to the basement to see Zach. He is lying on the floor wrapped in a quilt, like a giant draft stopper wedged against the door that leads out onto the lot. One of his hands is propped against the edge of the old Chambers oven. I nicknamed it the Swayze stove, because it had once belonged to the star of *Dirty Dancing*, who lived with his wife in this lower part of the house in the late 1970s. It sits disconnected, awaiting refurbishment. It feels odd to be thinking about Patrick Swayze at a time like this, and yet I do. My aunt once told me that Swayze, who was still a budding actor at that time, would drive to an overlook on Mulholland Drive at night, gaze at the city beneath him, and declare, "I am going to conquer you."

I say it now too, under my breath, and I clench my fists, ready to battle for my son.

4

PRETTY BOY

"One more question," the doctor says. "Was it a normal birth? A healthy pregnancy?"

His teeth are white and evenly spaced, reminding me of the man in the Colgate commercial. I feel the plush cushions underneath me, hear the hum of the air conditioner. I try to think. Hard. The smell of his expensive cologne is so strong I can taste it.

It seems like a legitimate question.

I look at Zach. His body is tipped forward in the chair across from us, his eyes fixed on the patterned carpet. He asks if it is the same one that we had in our London home, if it has been brought here. I can't follow his trail of thought, but I force a smile and say, "No, Zigs, I don't think it can be." Nance looks at me quizzically, reminding me that the doctor is waiting for my response.

"I think it was quite normal," I say, neglecting to mention the fact that my stepfather died when I was just a few weeks short of delivering Zach.

I also fail to mention Albert the cat. We got him when I was a couple of months along with Zach. I have read that pregnant women's antibody response to toxoplasmosis doubles or triples the risk of psychosis to the fetus. It can be caught quite easily from under-cooked meat, unwashed hands or handling cat litter. Could I have touched the little gray clumps of waste while emptying Albert's tray, and failed to wash my hands properly? What about the raw chicken breasts I cut into slivers to make the curry we all loved so much? Did I contaminate my unborn child *in utero*? More irrational thoughts are brewing in me like beer in a keg. There are higher rates of psychosis in those born in the city. Winter babies are more prone. Zach was delivered in London in November.

"Yes, yes, I believe it was normal," I reiterate, because the links I have read about seem so absurd to me right now.

This doctor won't be the last to ask such intimate questions. Therapists will bring up the subject too, and it will sometimes appear as part of a tick-box questionnaire on the intake paperwork at the mental health clinics. In time there will be more and more research done on prenatal and perinatal depression and how this can affect the development of a baby.

The suite where we are gathered today is twelve floors above the Wilshire Corridor in West Los Angeles. I look out to the Santa Monica Mountains and the Pacific Palisades. A picture-postcard view that strikes me as surreal, considering our suffering. Zach is not feeling better. It is five or six weeks since his release from the ward, and this private psychiatric consultation is costing us four hundred dollars for the hour. It is the second opinion that I hope will give us some answers. It is a desperate attempt to gain an understanding of what is happening and why, to find some drugs that will do more than just sedate Zach and make his appetite voracious. I am hoping for a new label for Zach, something more socially acceptable, less stigmatized—like that of General Anxiety.

It is quite a feat that we made it here at all. Zach spent this morning—as he has so many others since his discharge from the ward—preoccupied with his interior world. It is as if there is so much going on in his mind that he cannot move his body, so he freezes under the stucco arch doorway between the living room and the garden. He looks at himself for minutes at a time in the big mirror on the wall of the porch, his brows furrowed, his expression perplexed.

Perhaps I could rouse him from this momentary kind of stillness by touching his arm, or putting an LP on the vintage record player, as if presiding over a party game of musical statues like I did when he was little. But I can't switch gears. There is a growing sense of madness in me too. It is a state of mind that keeps me rooted in my chair, a notebook on the table in front of me, documenting his movements, his moods, his many hours spent either sleeping or eating. But what if we are not the only ones? What if we are all mad to an extent, on a spectrum of disorder? How could we not be, if we consider the state of the world that we live in?

It won't be long before I find out that there are new categories of madness created each year and written into the diagnostic statistical manual, the bible that is used by psychiatrists to diagnose their patients. These classifications earn the psychiatric and pharmaceutical industry a lot of money, because they legitimize the fact that these states are disorders of the brain that need treatment with drugs.

This particular private assessment at the luxury office on Wilshire Boulevard will label Zach with a different diagnosis, but it is just as grave, if not more so, than the original one. Schizoaffective disorder is described by psychiatrists as a complex condition which includes the altered states present in schizophrenia and the drastic shifts in mood present in bipolar experiences. This diagnosis will make me balk, dry my mouth—not just because there will be twice as much for me to learn about, but because people fear the word *schizophrenia*, including me and Zach and almost everyone I know. It comes from the Greek, and combines *schizein* ("split") and *phren* ("mind").

Short of bribing the doctor in exchange for a more acceptable diagnosis, I can't think of anything else to say other than, "Are you sure?" Soon enough it will be a moot point anyway, because another psychiatrist will classify Zach as having paranoid schizophrenia, and the one after that will suggest he has depression with psychotic features. The classifications are as changeable as his mood, or as illustrative of the mutability in the field of psychiatry. One thing that every diagnosis has in common is the fact that there is no scientific medical test to prove anything, and nobody seems to know for sure what is really going on. It is guesswork, trial and error, more like a game of spin-the-bottle than science.

The mental health campaigner Will Hall once said, "When doctors diagnosed me with schizophrenia, they weren't revealing something inside of me, they were casting a spell and imposing something on me. It was my job to break that spell."

·

"Was it a normal birth?"

The doctor's question stays with me long after we leave his office.

If it happened to have been Dale experiencing extreme distress, it might have made some semblance of sense. His birth was anything but normal. I was supine, numb and at the mercy of the obstetrician who vacuumed him from my retroverted womb after attaching a suction cap to his head. My first son's spine against my spine, with no fluid left to ease his passage into the world, both of us torn and bruised and crying afterward. All my carefully written birth-plan notes dashed with drugs and interventions and an authority that I could not fight. And yet, despite such a traumatic birth, a low Apgar score and a stay in the special care baby unit, Dale does not have these experiences of an altered state. Dale is not labeled as psychotic.

When Zach was born, it was different. I was in charge. I danced drug-free around the delivery suite at Whipps Cross Hospital in London's East End. The room was windowless, lit by fluorescent strips. A large clock hung on the white wall, the gleam of surgical steel and apparatus was everywhere. There was less intervention than I had had the first time around. There didn't seem to be any other staff around, except the midwife, or if there were, I was too tuned inward to notice their presence.

As I moved, hour after hour, in a hip-swaying trance, Zach's father, Gordon, and the midwife strained to keep up with me. The two of them must have been worried that the baby was going to be born onto the floor amid all my gyrating and primeval grunting, so they stopped me, the midwife placing one hand on my shoulder to still the rhythm of my footwork, and the other between my thighs, blindly probing my cervix.

"She's ready," she said to Gordon, as if I was fresh out of the oven, like a prime belly of pork. The midwife wrapped a firm arm around my waist and cajoled me toward the hospital bed. "You're crowning. It'll be safer for the baby to deliver you up here." She patted the bed and then my buttocks as I climbed up onto starched white sheets and a giant paper towel that rustled beneath me.

I knelt, even though that made it harder for the midwife to do her job, and I screamed, despite her tapping my leg and asking me to stop.

"You'll scare the other women, making noise like that."

Gordon held my hips so that I didn't topple from the bed.

———

That second birth was hard, but it was all mine, every inch of burning agony. As I felt the baby slide from me, I smiled. I had my girl. A daughter.

"It's a little boy, love. We have another son." It was Gordon's voice, cutting through my elation. I groaned as I made the final push to deliver the placenta. I felt a wave of disappointment wash over my tired body.

"He's lovely," the midwife said.

I remember Gordon's pallor under the light, his eyes narrow and weary as he held the swaddled baby to his chest. "He looks like you, love. Look, he has a really big nose." He did, and an ample head of hair, almost too much for something so new. In just nine months of living inside me he had grown to look like a little old man.

"I already have a boy. I was meant to have a daughter this time."

The midwife stopped her duties and furrowed her brow.

"Now look here," she said, in an Irish accent. "There are some mothers who lose their babies, or their babies are born very sick. You have a lovely healthy son, don't be ungrateful."

She took the baby from Gordon, unwrapped him and placed him on my stomach. He moved his head, rooting for food, then sank into me as if I were the giant beanbag in mum's living room, its contents spilled and settled over the years.

After eight hours of labor, he was all slippery newness. I touched him gingerly, stroked his wave of wet, dark hair. He made more of a coo than a cry. I felt a stirring in me. He was so soft in my arms.

In my mind, I had painted a scene of going back to Chingford Hall, the estate I lived on with Gordon, and proudly announcing to the neighbors, *It's a girl! I have one of each—that's it, now. I'm done.* But with my son in my arms, the canvas changed. I added a new layer. I had two little boys. Brothers. My daughter would have been called Anastasia or Artemisia; Ana or Arti for short. But now I needed a name for my son.

"What do you think of Jeremiah, or Jedediah?" I asked when my younger sister Zoë came to visit us. She screwed up her nose as if there was a bad smell in the ward.

"What about Zedakiah, or Zebadiah?" I said, warming to my theme, looking specifically at my sister for moral support. "I want a name with a Z in it, like yours. It's unusual." She and Gordon both looked at me. Zoë, disbelieving, her head cocked to one side, stared at the back of the baby's head, at all that hair, as if willing one of the names to fit him.

"Zacharius?" I asked.

"Yes!" Zoë shouted, as if she had won the pools. "Zachary for short." She shook my hand, making it a deal I couldn't go back on.

Gordon grabbed the baby-naming book from the birthing bag. He flicked to the last page.

"Zacharius, from Zechariah. Hebrew. The Lord remembers."

"She's gone all religious on us," Zoë said.

"I haven't. It just came to me."

•

I was just nineteen when I met Gordon. He had steely blue eyes, thin blonde hair and an accent like Jack Duckworth's in *Coronation Street*. I had recently graduated from high school with two low-grade GCSEs. Although I'd studied woodwork and metalwork with the boys, and they had joined me for cookery and needlework, the emphasis was clearly on us girls making babies and cakes, and leaving the mortise-and-tenon joints up to the lads.

In the beginning, before the children came along, Gordon introduced me to Boddingtons, mushy peas and the fact that Karl

Marx was an economist and not, to my amazement, Harpo and Chico's brother.

I looked for the good in him. His name alone, Gordon Thomas Chadwick, had so many syllables—it sounded important. He told me his surname was of Anglo-Saxon and Norse origin, inspiring him to paint scenes of Viking longboats and warriors, which he did at the weekends. I joined him and watched him squatting in front of his canvas, paintbrush in hand, a cigarette dangling from his mouth and a halo of smoke above his head. I willed myself to love Gordon and everything about him in those early days, running to keep up with him when we were out walking, and laughing at his jokes even if I didn't understand them. I spent more and more time with him in his little bedsit that was paid for by the council as part of his social work training package. I would make my mother happy. No question.

Most of my friends had already had babies. I knew it was my turn to go next. It wasn't long before I forgot to take my contraceptive pill and got pregnant. Maybe I did it on purpose, subconsciously, to be an obedient daughter. It was 1987. I was twenty-one years old.

•

When the community midwife came out to weigh Zach, and make sure I was recovering, she must have realized that my demeanor was a bit off. Two years earlier, after giving birth to Dale, my postpartum hormones had gotten out of whack, and I was swallowed up by insomnia and crying fits.

"I'm doing much better this time, sister," I told the midwife. "I'm keeping myself together for the sake of the little ones."

"That's good," she replied, "but the baby blues are very common—just like before, you might need a little bit of help." She wrote me a prescription, then reached into her satchel for a blister pack of white, greasy nubs—progesterone suppositories.

"Thank you," I said, trusting her instinct. She was a professional. She saw women like me all the time.

I positioned Zach in his baby sling and moved to the window. I watched the midwife leave the tower block on her bicycle, riding freely down the ramp to visit the next new mother. Zach was still, his ear against my heart. I had held Dale up at this very same spot when he was newly born and helpless. But it was so different back then. Now there was nothing but wasteground beside the reservoir where the travelers used to live. Gone were the caravans sitting in a ring, dogs chained up outside.

Gordon, sensing my restlessness, sidled up close one evening as I sat breastfeeding Zach on the couch.

"Will you marry me?" he asked, rubbing Zach's back, circling the soft brushed cotton of his onesie. It was matter-of-fact, no pomp or ceremony.

"We'll see," I said, competing with the television in the background. When I was growing up, *We'll see* had always been a euphemism for "no," a cowardly, non-committal way of biding time.

•

Back at the house in Los Angeles, Zach moves with a slow, awkward gait. I recall him first learning to walk, toddling around our flat. Then there was the odd shuffle we did some years later when I was in a hurry for work: Zach hoisted onto my hip, weighing me down and making me lopsided as we moved together through the school playground. I remember his giggle and shrill cries of "Mummy!" like one of those little dolls that squeaked when it was turned upside down.

It hurts my chest to think of these times, and I am not entirely sure why. I can remember him on those winter mornings, in his gray duffel coat with the wooden toggles. My Paddington Bear, with his burnished hair and jagged little fringe. Have I already started to romanticize the past?

Long after Zach has gone to sleep, I am still reading. Nance has taken to donning an eye mask to block out the light from my computer. I trawl google searches for answers, but Zach's new diagnosis of schizoaffective disorder shows up on almost every website as a "life-limiting, chronic disability." I fall into a rabbit hole that leads me from schizoaffective disorder to schizophrenia to paranoid schizophrenia.

The theories on what may have led Zach to detach from consensual reality are complex and seemingly infinite. I will need to revisit them, one by one, to scrutinize each factor like a jury weighing up a criminal case. For now, though, I must simply get them all down, worried that if I miss something it might be the one definitive cause of what he's experiencing, and as such the answers will evade me forever.

The sound of pattering footsteps intrudes. Our bedroom door clicks open. It is Zach, bathed in shadow. He may have been crying, but I can't be certain. The alarm clock next to Nance's side of the bed says 3 a.m. She is a light sleeper, and I don't want to disturb her, so I press my finger to my mouth, and pat my side of the mattress. Zach sits next to me, still dressed in yesterday's shorts and a soft flannel shirt.

"Are you scared of the Big One?" he asks, a Californian term for the earthquake that is predicted to come one day, though nobody knows quite when.

"No, I'm not," I tell him. "This house is built on bedrock. It survived the 1994 Northridge quake."

It's a new thing, his fear of earthquakes. He never cared about us living on the San Andreas Fault before now. His apprehension is misplaced anyway, I think, because at a gut level I feel we've already been hit, that a large chasm has opened up in our family landscape. I have no idea how to go about bridging that gap.

He leaves momentarily, then returns with his quilt. He lays it on the floor of our bedroom, crawls underneath and closes his eyes. The moon shines through the window, illuminating his face like a spotlight. He's a grown man now, but I feel the urge to swaddle him.

Somehow, exhaustion claims me for the next four hours and I sleep deeply. The moon gives way to the sun seeping through the sheers, waking me to a new day. I clamber out of bed and crouch beside Zach, who is still asleep on our bedroom floor. I remember how as a child he liked me to comb my fingers through his curly hair and scratch his scalp. I used to watch the boys as they slept, thinking that if I loved them enough, I could stop anything bad from happening to them.

But now—now, I circle the idea that this could have been the problem, that I might have loved Zach too much. In the 1940s, psychiatrist Frieda Fromm-Reichmann proposed the theory that mothers like me, who had children with a schizophrenia diagnosis, were schizophrenogenic, or somehow to blame. Fromm-Reichmann clinically defined us mothers as dominant, overprotective but basically rejecting. I realize part of me desperately wants this archaic notion to be true still. If something I have done has caused my son's mind to supposedly short-circuit, flood with dopamine and lose cognitive function and short-term memory, then surely a change on my part would suffice to cure him.

I stare at Zach's broad forehead. Is it true that neurons are misfiring in his pre-frontal lobe, or is that just another hypothesis? I pull the cover up to his chin and stroke his forehead: warm, as if something is cooking in his mind. "It's going to be okay, baby," I whisper.

Baby—all five feet nine inches and one hundred and sixty pounds of him.

5

TRANSPLANT

In the evenings after school in London, nine-year-old Zach played *The Legend of Zelda: Ocarina of Time* on his Nintendo 64. He would stick the tip of his tongue in the gap between his upper front teeth to help him concentrate. As well as gappy teeth, he had astigmatism and was extremely far-sighted. He wore blue, plastic-framed NHS glasses with a patch on the left lens, making him look like my very own Harry Potter.

I could never have anticipated how distinct from each other the boys would be. It was as if I had borne one child for each of us: Dale, with his fair hair, cerulean blue eyes, tall, wiry build and exuberance, was like Gordon. Zach, a placid, observant child with chestnut hair, eyes the color of agave and a shorter, plumper frame was the image of me.

Despite the differences between my sons, and how hard it was to be everything to the two of them, I somehow knew in a deep, unspoken way that the day would come when I would go it alone as a single parent. Perhaps it was the pattern of the past, of history repeating itself. My mother, her mother before her. All of us left by our menfolk. Or the fact that on Chingford Hall there were more of us women on our own with our kids than there were those who had partners or husbands.

There were two things that were different about me, though,

that made me stand out from the crowd, that set me apart from my female ancestors. One was the fact that I had defied everything and everyone, climbed above my station, despite all odds, to start university. The other was the fact that I had fallen in love with a woman.

There were only two lesbians on the estate as far as I knew, Big Jen and Pauline. They sat outside the Greyhound drinking ale and fighting. They were a spectacle. I wasn't gay like them. My girlfriend—a fellow student from my Women's Studies course—was pretty with copper-colored hair and matching lipstick. I slept with her for the first time in the late winter of 1991, then crept back to Chingford Hall the next morning with two-year-old Zach in my arms. Gordon was waiting for me in the living room. He had been pacing most of the night, making tracks in the poorly laid brown carpet. I didn't lie. I couldn't. It was clear how smitten I was with this new love. "I bloody told you those classes would turn you into a lesbian," Gordon said. He shook his head, his thin flyaway hair almost transparent in the cold early light.

Dale woke up and found us. He put his small boy arms around his dad's legs, and we stayed like that, the four of us, opponents in a ring, two against two.

I was taking a gamble by following my heart, by loving a woman. The risk was enormous, but the flutter in my belly was big and growing, an infatuation of gale-force strength enough to knock me off my feet.

I couldn't ignore how we had been thrown together, Gordon and I, by the expectations of our parents, by me getting pregnant, by seeing this life as the norm.

I watched him, the father of our boys, pack the tan leather case that he kept on top of the wardrobe and walk out of the door, leaving the three of us behind.

I was twenty-six years old. Dale was four. Zach was two.

It wasn't only Gordon that left our relationship. I had no doubt departed long before, vacating our partnership emotionally, sexually. Was I making history rather than repeating it? I didn't even consider that we might have been able to fix us, work it out, give it another go. How was that possible when I was gay?

Mum helped me after Gordon and I separated, watching the boys so that I could continue to study and get my degree. I recall those early years after graduating, I'd steered Dale's excess energy toward football. Zach, however, had stayed closer to home and to me, collecting books and Pokémon cards, and attending the infant chess group after school on Tuesday afternoons. Some evenings he set the board up on the cluttered kitchen table and tried to teach me the game, but I wasn't adept at holding all the moves in my head—I was occupied by the things I needed to do for my job, that I had secured straight out of university, as a college lecturer: the marking, the lesson plans, the prep. Chess seemed so alien to me and my working-class roots. Chess and Shakespeare—I had never taken to either of them. Over and over, I asked him, "Now what do the knights do again, how do they move? And the castle?"

"It's a rook," he said impatiently, spelling out the number of squares the piece could hop forward or backward or side-to-side, and by the time it was my turn I had forgotten once again.

"Can't we play checkers? I love checkers. It's so much easier to remember the rules, and I don't have a lot of time."

"No," he said, writing down the basic moves for me.

In 1999, he qualified to take part in the Essex chess tournament at Butlins Holiday Camp in Bognor Regis. I was so proud, I told everyone I knew. A spot of overtime meant I could pay for him to participate, and for my sister Zoë and her son Braedon to join us. Zach was especially protective of his quirky cousin Brae, who was a year younger than him and had been diagnosed with autism. The two of them were more like brothers than cousins. Brae looked up to Zach with an admiration that was clear to see. They had a closeness and an understanding that went above and beyond labels, and where Brae did or didn't fit on the autism spectrum. They were just themselves, two boys who liked the same things: Dragon Ball Z and Pikachu.

Zach won every chess match in his age group over the course of the weekend at Butlins. I ruffled his hair and said, "That's amazing, Zigs." Despite how hard the day-to-day was for us financially, and how tired I was as a single parent, this quiet triumph made me glow.

On the day of the awards I stood quietly at the back of the hall, keeping one eye on Braedon who was flapping his arms and circling the room, distressed by the clapping and cheering, and the other on Zoë, who was trying to placate him without much luck. Just when I thought we might have to leave, Zach grinned cheekily at me—that striking gap visible between his top front teeth—and he marched down from the stage toward his cousin like a king penguin, tucking Braedon under his wing and squeezing him hard. He whispered something in his ear before returning to the ceremony. I watched my nephew close his eyes, then move to the front row, where he sat down cross-legged, gazing up at Zach.

As happy as I was to see my boy win the tournament, I was more chuffed to witness the bond he shared with his cousin. These boys really had each other's backs, two sensitive souls. Zach and Brae. A team. Maybe they were both wired in a similar way, and differently from most of their peers. We might call it neurodivergence, this thing that set them apart. The very simple fact that we all come in many different forms.

Growing up I didn't have any female cousins, but I was tethered to Zoë. Nine years younger than me, I had begged for her to be born, and mothered her ever since. I knew the value of Zach and Braedon's rapport. Breaking them apart would be unthinkable.

·

It was almost three years after the tournament when the phone woke me just before dawn. I rushed to the kitchen, hoping the noise wouldn't disturb the boys. It was April 1, 2001, but this was no April Fool's prank. It was Dennis and Deirdre, two of my Auntie Betty's closest neighbors, eight hours behind me in Los Angeles. This auntie, who was gay, lived in the Hollywood Hills and worked for Irwin Allen at 20th Century Fox, was my mum's auntie, not mine. She had fostered mum from the Norwood Jewish Orphanage after the Second World War. By rights we should have called her Grandma, but I tried that once and she said, "Oh no, darling, that makes me feel much too old."

I leaned in to the receiver to learn that Auntie Betty needed help. She was becoming frail, and her memory was compromised. She failed to recall most details these days aside from one important thing—what would happen to her estate after her demise.

"Did you know that she has left you almost everything in her will?" the neighbors asked me. I didn't, and the unsociable hour of the call made the idea even more surreal.

"A lot of vulnerable people get taken advantage of if they live alone," they said. "We think she needs your help. Could you come here?"

Outside, the moon was waxing, framed perfectly in the upper right corner of the window. I watched it glow. "I have a job here," I explained, my voice thin and scratchy from sleep. "The boys, responsibility. I'm not sure how I can help." After replacing the receiver neatly in its cradle, I refilled my hot water bottle at the sink and hugged it to my chest for a long time. Dale woke first, and I heard him puttering along the hallway.

The next half an hour, as usual, was taken up with breakfast, uniforms, the packing of bags (theirs and mine), books and lunches. The search for door keys, shoes, coats and the flat-head screwdriver I used to start the rusty old Triumph Toledo, a car I had bought for sixty pounds that came without an ignition barrel or key. Lastly, there was the routine jostling as the boys bickered over whose turn it was to sit up front with me in the car.

At a red light, I observed the two of them. Dale was having a growth spurt. His voice broke when he sang, and there was faint blonde fuzz above his upper lip. Zach was already wider than Dale, stockier, sturdier, able to stand up for himself when they fought. His hair—darker, thicker and unruly in the way it framed his face— along with his glasses that were always in need of a polish, made him seem more cut off from the morning; half asleep, or still waking up. I wanted the best for my sons. I always had. It was just that the wanting had been quashed by fatigue and reality—until now.

After dropping them off at the school gates, I wondered *why me*? Why was I the beneficiary? Why not mum? She was Elizabeth's surrogate daughter. Besides, I had already prospered from my aunt's generosity. There had been cards, presents and dollar bills to exchange at the bank. For my eleventh birthday, Auntie had bought me a diary that locked with a key, which I treasured. The following Christmas she sent me a brown ViewMaster and a set of slides. On Sundays, when the weather was too rotten to play outside, I lay on my back on the living room floor, pointed the toy at the ceiling light and brought the iconic images to life. Mickey and Minnie waving to me from Disneyland. The Golden Gate Bridge glinting in the sun in

San Francisco. The Grand Canyon, which I was told could be seen from space. This was the America I had learned to love from technicolor musicals and Disney animations.

At the Green Man roundabout, the sky darkened and it started to rain. My wipers—worn down to the metal—screeched across the windshield. I had been waiting for payday to get a new set.

The idea of inheriting a small fortune was so foreign to me. What would it do to my relationship with my siblings? Would I share my inheritance with them and feel forever benevolent? Would I keep it, and feel somewhat singled out and ashamed? And what was it? How much? It made me feel nervous. It made me feel greedy.

Being broke was part of my identity. Mum had brought me up to berate the snobs in North Chingford, to know the worth of the working class, down-to-earth folk who'd give you the shirts off their backs.

In the classroom I wrote an essay topic on the whiteboard, and as my students buried their heads in their notebooks, I felt myself being pulled back into the past, fantasizing like I used to about the distant land where Auntie Betty—my fairy godmother—awaited me in this rags-to-riches tale.

My life as a single parent, rushing from one part-time teaching job to the next, staying up late to get through marking and preparation for the next day, left me exhausted and disillusioned. I knew this was a huge decision, but I was ready. Poised at the fork in the road, about to take a journey that would transform us completely, irrevocably—and, in my very firm belief, for the best.

•

Dale was thirteen, Zach was eleven when I steered them and our luggage through the international terminal at London Heathrow, bound for Los Angeles. Stepping onto the enormous aircraft, I tapped the outer shell of the plane—three times, my lucky number—right above the wing. We took our seats in the upper deck, ready to be rocketed from one side of the pond to the other—5,437 miles as the crow flies. A world away from jacket potatoes, cheese and beans, and HP sauce; from tikka masala, Marmite on toast, BBC Radio 4, mum. Dale's eyes were wide with anticipation, his energy thrumming like the jet engines. "How far is it?" he asked before we even took off. Zach found his pillow and settled in with his new Harry Potter book, focusing intently on the page.

On the other side of the window, the London sky turned gray and a light drizzle dampened the tarmac. I wondered what it might be like to live in a temperate climate where it wasn't always raining. As the plane started to taxi, I felt it in my stomach—the enormity of taking my children so far away. Once airborne, we flew over the River Thames and I said a silent goodbye to Chingford Hall Estate, the North Circular Road, the polluted River Lea, the past.

When we disembarked in Los Angeles it was sunny, as it was almost all year round. Auntie Betty, ninety-one and almost childlike in the way she lived in the moment and forgot everything else, connected instantly with the boys.

"Oh darling, I'm so glad you're here. Now how do I know you again?"

We explored her home, clambering up a set of outdoor steps onto a flat rooftop with panoramic views. On one side of the canyon a pagoda rose from the hill. This was Yamashiro, a landmark built in the 1920s by two Jewish brothers to house their art collection, and now a restaurant. James Bond movies had been filmed there. To the north was the Hollywood Bowl, where we would go and watch a concert once the summer season started. Standing there with my boys on top of the tallest house at the crest of the hill, I knew that we would thrive. This was the land I had loved for so long, from afar through the lens of that old brown View-Master.

I took us all down to the basement. We kicked our shoes off, feeling the smooth, cool hardwood floor under our bare feet. Once unpacked, I made dinner on the antique Chambers stove. The boys and Auntie retired early. I ran a hot bath and reclined in the old enamel tub.

In less than a day we had crossed the Atlantic and landed in a new place, swapping the end of one era for the beginning of another. There was no knowing what we would encounter here, whether we would stay or leave, but in that moment I felt intrepid, brave, alone, yet connected to the long line of my Jewish ancestors who had left the old country to make for the new, wanting something better.

6

RENAISSANCE MAN OF THE YEAR

"I can do it," Zach insists, propping himself up on one elbow on his bed, where he continues to spend almost all day sleeping. It has been almost five months since he was discharged from the psych ward and had to take medical leave from UCLA. His laptop hums as he inspects the curriculum for the next quarter.

I am busy too, sizing up his beard. His facial hair has become our barometer. When he is feeling resilient he transforms himself into a fresh-faced, clean-shaven guy, someone who is ready to take another stab at interacting with the world. When he is depressed, he lets his beard grow bushy and unkempt. Today it is somewhere in between the two. I see the flecks of ginger from his father's side. Despite his inner turmoil, he is so good-looking.

In high school, Zach loved music, theater, science and art. His aptitude for these subjects won him a qualification: Renaissance Man of the Year. I should frame that thing and hang it on the wall. Mum used to do that with our certificates. She chose the bathroom, displaying our merits above the toilet. She insisted they would be seen more that way.

"There are some classes online," Zach tells me. "Not enough to give me the credits I need. I have to take some in-person units." The assignments and final grade relied on in-class student participation.

Missing just a couple of classes could mean the difference between him passing or failing.

Zach's recent withdrawal from his studies after his release from the hospital is still fresh in my memory: the interviews with his academic counselor, the copious amounts of paperwork, the bureaucracy involving future funding, grades and health insurance. It was exhausting.

"Mum, don't worry," he says, looking at my tense expression. "I'll take classes that start later in the day. I have to get my degree. I worked so hard to get to UCLA."

"I know you did darling," I tell him. "I'm so proud of you."

He returns to studying the schedules and I try to turn it all around and visualize him upright and tall, striding across the campus, his self-esteem and friendships blossoming again.

Invested more than ever in finding success stories, I scour the internet to see who has managed such a feat in this part of the world. There are lists of historical figures who supposedly lived with dyslexia. Einstein, Leonardo da Vinci, Edison. I want to find a similar account of individuals who have returned to university after a psychotic episode and gone on to complete their degree. After many evenings sat in front of my computer, I find her: an author and advocate for mental health reform, with lived experience of a diagnosis of schizophrenia. Her name is Ellyn Saks. She has a bachelor's, a master's and a PhD.

I order a second-hand copy of her memoir, *The Center Cannot Hold: My Journey Through Madness*. I read it late at night, my bedside lamp shining on the dog-eared pages. Nance sleeps next to me, but I am hardly aware of her. It is Ellyn I am spending the night with. She draws me into her world. I am in equal parts dismayed by the horrors and in awe of her skill at narration.

I have to meet this Ellyn Saks. She is linked to my mother country (she had her first altered state while studying at the University
of Oxford). She is what is known in the Los Angeles mental health
community as "high functioning," even though this is a term that
will soon be outmoded. She credits the English psychoanalyst that
she saw daily during her time in the UK as being crucial to aid-
ing her recovery. I want to know what and who else made her well
enough to become a Dean of the Law Department at the University of Southern California, to become a *New York Times* bestselling
author and to have her own TED Talk. Zach has what his psychiatrist terms "plenty of cognitive reserve." It means he is smart, at least
at this moment in time. Most Western physicians and psychiatrists,
however, subscribe to what is called the biomedical model, which
holds that living with schizoaffective disorder may compromise
Zach's cognition in the future. They believe that psychosis affects
brain matter and neuronal connectivity, and that each psychotic
break generates a kind of inflammatory response and neurological
toxicity. They consider antipsychotic medication protective and suggest that if mentally ill patients don't remain on medication for life,
they may lose their ability to study, to remember, to read—both in
terms of motivation and intellectual capacity.

This theory, like all theories, is heavily debated. Studies by the
opposing camp show that it is hard to really tell what psychosis
does because of the harm antipsychotic drugs can do to the brain.
These researchers take trauma into consideration and may interpret hearing voices or experiencing extreme states as existential or
spiritual crises.

Most days, I am confused, not sure what to believe. The biomedical or broken brain model frightens me. I am a teacher by trade: my
life is built upon books and theses and knowledge, and I had hoped
that Zach would follow suit.

I wonder if Ellyn Saks takes powerful antipsychotic drugs. I email her and tell her about my plight, how much I would love to take Zach to meet her, how she would inspire him and show him what is possible, rather than what isn't. Miraculously, she agrees to meet us in a restaurant near the University of Southern California.

On the day that we are meant to convene, Zach sneezes and says that his body aches. He doesn't feel well enough to come with me. I make him a hot honey and lemon drink and leave without him, disappointed but unwilling to forego the opportunity. I get into the car, but something in me makes it hard to back out of the drive-way. It is fear. Presenting as flu-like symptoms, one of the more dangerous side effects of the drugs that Zach takes is neuroleptic malignant syndrome (NMS), a rare but serious condition, caused by a rise in serotonin levels, that can lead to death. I have put it out of my mind until now, but suddenly the thought is crushing, a boulder on my chest. I know I am meant to stay alert for signs of high fever, confusion, sweating and changes in pulse, heart rate and blood pressure.

As I make my way downtown, I calculate the other long-term health risks of antipsychotics that I have read about, including increases in blood sugar levels and changes in cholesterol and triglyceride—this is known as metabolic syndrome. Most disturbing of all is the susceptibility to uncontrollable movements of face, tongue or other parts of the body, known as tardive dyskinesia, which can be permanent. People with a diagnosis of schizophrenia die on average twenty-five years earlier than the rest of the population. This is largely thought to be due to the physical toll that long-term antipsychotics take on the body.

There is evidence that those who have had adverse experiences in childhood die earlier too. There are higher levels of addiction to alcohol and drugs in this demographic, perhaps to numb trauma.

It all comes rushing at me in this moment, the facts and figures so vivid it is as if I have swallowed an encyclopedia entry on the subject and retained every line. Thankfully Zach isn't with me, because the realization that when he is my age he may be living the last few years of his life makes me cry.

Parked up at my destination, I look at my watch, wipe my eyes on the back of my hands and call Zach.

"I feel a lot better," he says. "What is there to eat?" I let my breath out all the way and lean back to be cradled by the headrest. There are some leftovers in the fridge, I tell him. I see him smile in my mind's eye; I feel like I can even hear it in his voice before he says goodbye.

The café where Ellyn and I have arranged to meet is a bright and busy Americana venue that smells of fried food and Folgers. I don't understand how anyone can drink coffee that smells like old cigarette butts, let alone order free refills of the stuff, but regardless of the aroma, I like the décor—the Formica-top tables and red leatherette seats.

When she enters, I recognize her from her TED Talk. She is tall and thin, and her hair is gray and untamed. I am immediately heartened by the fact that she isn't overweight—maybe Zach will be able to avoid the metabolic syndrome caused by the drugs and maintain a healthy weight. We sit opposite each other in a booth at the back. Ellyn orders a Cobb salad with dressing on the side, which she uses sparingly.

"I come here every day, so they know me. I always order the same thing," she admits. She also confesses that she is a workaholic, and that routine is extremely important to her because it keeps her stable.

"When my husband and I go away on holiday, it's for very short periods, and I often have to take work with me," she says.

Husband—she is married. I wonder if Zach will ever get married. Not that long ago people with a diagnosis of schizophrenia, including Ellyn, were told that they would never marry, never work, and must be permanently medicated, sheltered or institutionalized.

"Do you have a passion outside of work?" I ask.

"I roller-skate at Exposition Park," she says, and she smiles so faintly I almost miss it.

I smile back, imagining the resilient Ellyn skating, her hair billowing out behind her as she glides through the park, past the Los Angeles Memorial Coliseum, the Natural History Museum of Los Angeles County and the California Science Center. What a fitting locale to work out in, I think—a place that combines intellect and freedom.

"I so wanted Zach to come with me, but he didn't feel well," I tell her.

"I'm sorry," she says, and I know she is, because she looks at me earnestly and puts her fork down.

She has been through trauma. During one of her hospitalizations she was placed in restraints and forcibly medicated. As a result of such treatment, she advocates fiercely for better care, for understanding, for change.

"Don't ever give up hope," she tells me.

"My son is high-functioning, according to his psychiatrist," I tell Ellyn, as if this somehow puts us in a separate club, a sub-group within a sub-group. Ellyn has been researching people who fall into this category. She has met with successful Los Angeles-based technicians; legal, business and medical professionals; people with a diagnosis of schizophrenia who are able to manage their altered states while working toward college degrees.

What I learn that afternoon, and what I take home with me, is that Ellyn Saks does indeed take antipsychotics. Alongside the drugs she has routine, responsibility, a healthy diet, exercise and a life partner that has empathy. I am buoyed by the way that Ellyn has managed to achieve so much. She is a role model for families like mine.

"Ellyn Saks is amazing," I say to Zach later that evening. "You are going to be too. You are already."

After supper, Nance calls me from her parents' house, where she stays when she is working from the San Francisco Bay area. I tell her about my meeting with Ellyn.

"Wow, hon," she says. "If Zach can just manage the voices, learn to live with them . . ."

After the call, I leash the dogs and ask Zach if he wants to join me walking around the neighborhood. He does, and we tread silently around Paramount Drive, down the secret stairs—as they are referred to—that lead onto Glencoe.

"This is so good for us, Zigs." These are the only words I say, but I believe them entirely. I listen to my breath, to the soft clipclop of Belle's and Suki's claws on the sidewalk. The night is warm, and the sweet smell of citrus fruit is abundant. We are in synchrony as we walk, my boy and I, with the dogs sandwiched between us. It strikes me how much I want him to join Ellyn's sub-group, to be hailed as a miracle by his psychiatrist.

Surely in Los Angeles of all places, in 2010, with the cost of college tuition running to the tune of about ten thousand dollars per quarter, there should be adequate provision in place to help Zach. I make up my mind to pop into the office for students with disabilities, to ensure that he gets proper support, and that he has every chance of success.

Zach settles on a class that starts early, because there is no other option that fulfills his requirements. The other two classes he arranges to take online. I buy him a loud alarm clock. To begin with he rises when it goes off and stumbles a few paces from the bed to the wardrobe, where he keeps it, a strategy he imposed upon himself to try to avoid hitting the snooze button and going back to sleep. I help by making him strong coffee and calling him several times, but when he begins to sleep through the frighteningly loud alarm and leave the coffee untouched on the side, it becomes taxing for both of us. His drugs have such strong sedative effects that even with caffeine, the noise of the alarm and the brightest sunlight blasting through Zach's window, he cannot wake up.

When I am able to I drive him to campus, but he can't focus, and he sleeps through the lectures and seminars. He is given a note-taker, and promised extra time and a separate room for the exams. We arm him with a skateboard to move quickly through the crowds on campus and a pair of high-quality noise-canceling headphones to lessen the triggering sounds in his midst. Zach is still unable to cope.

By week three, he has only managed to attend two of his in-person classes. By week five, his grade is seriously compromised by his absences and lack of participation. His support team, an academic counselor and Maya from the office for students with disabilities, are unable to offer him anymore accommodations, and suggest that he begins the process of withdrawal from the on-campus class. When he tells me that Maya can help him to officially make the changes, to manage the paperwork, keep his student health insurance and retain his funding, I exhale and say thank God. I am secretly disappointed, though, that there aren't more measures in place and that the ratio-nale is to help Zach withdraw rather than stay.

To manage his remaining course load, he Skypes with his dad every day. Gordon is a history buff and now retired from work. Together they discuss the material, and Gordon tests him on sub-jects for his mid-terms. I listen to the two of them converse. It opens a soft spot in me, a chance to put old wounds to one side. I am desperate for Zach to succeed, and I bring everyone and everything to the fight.

Zach's old middle-school teacher has become like family to us. She visits and helps her Zachary Moon, as she nicknamed him, to structure his essays. If I can keep my belief in him getting six more units of credit under his belt, and Zach can keep his promise to stay off the marijuana and see his therapist and psychiatrist, I think we may be able to pull it off. The effort is enormous, but it is worth every kilojoule of energy we expend.

He has to get a B grade or higher to continue receiving his scholarship. He has never got anything less than an A since starting high school. His grade point average was up in the range that only few students attain, and he took advance placement studies that gave him college credit before he even left school. But the effects of the antipsychotics are taking their toll, and he has to study for much longer now. I see the concentration etched onto his brows, and I know he recognizes the change in his academic abilities too.

A couple of weeks after the official end of the quarter, Zach comes into my room with his laptop open on his college home page. His results are in. He got a B+ for History of Ancient Rome and a B for History of the American Civil War. I am ecstatic.

"It means you can continue to get your funding, Zigs. I'm so proud of you," I beam.

"Stop, Mum," he interjects. "I'm not the same. My brain is damaged. I used to get As. You know that. This is so fucked up. It's the meds—I'm telling you."

I try to speak, but Zach talks over me, louder, more urgent, "Or someone is dosing me with poison. I can't even talk properly anymore. Don't pretend you don't notice me slurring. Whose side are you on? Seriously?"

"I'm on your side," I say defensively, feeling my face start to flush with panic. "And why on earth would you think that anyone would be trying to poison you?" He is pacing. The dogs are sensing the angst and whining with shared apprehension.

"Zach," I say, calmly but firmly. "It's okay, you don't have to go back."

His frantic mood de-escalates a notch or two. I want to tell him that he could maybe learn to be pleased with a B+, but it doesn't feel like the appropriate moment. I am starting to worry that there are fewer and fewer right times, and a part of me feels like it is unrealistic to have so much hope. Maybe we won't make Ellyn Saks's list after all. Zach decides to sit out the next quarter. Perhaps he doesn't fit at UCLA anymore. It's too big. Too anonymous. I know him. I know my highly sensitive son.

Zach is exhausted. It takes everything he has to acknowledge it and sit out the following quarter. We sidestep into another realm, one with different expectations. I wonder at this point if he will go back, if he will graduate, what it might mean if he doesn't.

7

SHIFTING DIAGNOSES

Alongside the shift in diagnosis from psychosis NOS to schizo-affective disorder, Zach was prescribed a different antipsychotic drug called Zyprexa. The doctor with the very white teeth and the office that looks out onto some of the most expensive real estate in the old country tells us improvement can take up to six weeks, but skipped the fact that the drugs may not help everyone. Thirty-four percent of those with Zach's diagnosis have what psychiatry calls "refractory" or "treatment-resistant" schizophrenia. This means that, despite the antipsychotic drugs, the extreme distress and voices continue. It is where I get my first glimmer that psychosis doesn't appear to have an organic cause after all.

Zach doesn't like the Zyprexa any more than the Abilify. In fact, he despises it. He says it causes muscle spasms and pain in his legs, blurs his vision so he can't read properly, and makes him tired and constipated. These are just the initial side effects. There will be more, but we do not know that yet.

In my desire to make everything better, I buy magnesium and tiger balm for his body aches, a bounty of fresh fruit and vegetables, and a pot of Senna to get things moving. We make an appointment with Dr. Wong, the optometrist on Sunset Boulevard.

"He probably needs a stronger correction," I tell the receptionist over the phone.

———————

Dr. Wong works on Saturdays, which is perfect, although I know deep down in a way I never knew before that nothing or nobody is truly perfect. Nance found this optometrist last year. She had wanted to treat Zach to contact lenses for his eighteenth birthday. Being able to ditch his glasses made surfing, basketball and charming the girls a lot easier.

The doctor greets us. I wonder what he thinks about the change in my boy. Gone are his soft contact lenses. He has reverted to his old glasses. They dangle from his face as he sits with his head bowed, as if he is praying. Maybe he is? I wouldn't blame him.

The doctor lowers his voice and beckons us to follow him. He is intuitive and kind. I wish he could be Zach's psychiatrist, or his therapist, or—dare I think it?—his father.

In the room where he conducts the eye tests, there are pictures of his three young daughters at Disneyland. I stare at them, thinking about how Zach was that little when we first came here, how we did that fantastic trip too.

Dr. Wong performs the examination, confirming that Zach's sight has not deteriorated. He suggests that Zach might want to wear his glasses more often to see if that will help. He asks if any new drugs have been prescribed, telling us that he has met other people who complain of blurred vision as a side effect of antipsychotics. Zach perks up in the knowledge that he is not alone; that it is real; that something in the drug could be affecting the way his brain tracks and processes the world around him, even if it doesn't show up in Dr. Wong's equipment.

"I seriously want to stop taking this shit. It's making me stupid as well as blind," Zach says on the way home.

I argue with him, reiterating how, according to the psychiatrist, the side effects are more pronounced in the beginning, and that things will improve if we give the drug more time.

"He is the doctor, after all," I say. "Surely he knows best?"

Each night, traipsing into Zach's room with a glass of water, I hold out the drugs. Zach's bookshelf is in my periphery, but I block it out. I focus on the little pill dispenser in my hand and not on the CS Lewis, Tolkien and JK Rowling stories that he once loved to read. He is unable to follow words on the page anymore, nor concentrate enough to retain the plot.

One night, during the pill-taking routine, Zach is so frustrated that he pushes the drinking glass up to my chin and says, "If it's that good, why don't you take it?"

His eyes are dark and furious, and his skin is sallow from so little sunshine.

Nance sees I am visibly shaken after the tussle.

"Maybe it is wrong to force him. I won't be around forever to police the drugs," I say. "If he is so averse to the side effects—and it is his body—then shouldn't it be his choice?"

It doesn't require much to persuade Nance—who rarely takes as much as an aspirin—to see Zach's point of view, especially in the beginning, when we were all novices, learning by doing. I ask Zach if he will wean down gradually, with medical supervision. It seems smart, given what I have read about the dangers of stopping the drugs cold turkey. Zach agrees to withdraw gradually, and I am hopeful.

I don't stop reading, stumbling across research from China where doses of antipsychotics were cut in half and the patients improved, and other cases in the USA where psychiatric drugs were used during acute phases of experiences of psychosis, then discontinued during periods of stability. These people tended to have better rates of recovery and long-term function.

I buy a pill-cutter and speak to Zach's doctor, but he is averse to the idea. I feel like the rope in a game of tug of war, pulled in both directions, but then Zach makes a firm decision—even if we can't—and throws his pills in the waste-paper basket, or under the bed, or anywhere other than in his mouth. His mind is made up, and no amount of strong-arming or forestalling will change it. He is a stubborn Scorpio with a sting in his tail. Nance thinks it is this very determination that will get him through this, that will bring him back to us.

A few days go by. I watch him meticulously whenever I am home. Could he be right? Is discarding the antipsychotic drugs the answer? It is hard to know, because many of the people who manage to live a life without drugs do not stay within the system and so are not part of the statistical record. The research is skewed.

Within a very short period, he is most definitely less sedated. In the evenings we take the dogs out together, keeping in step for the two-mile loop, pushing ourselves up the steep section of North Sycamore Avenue, passing the iconic Magic Castle with its turrets and spires and lead glass windows. Zach talks in the future tense, of wanting to go back to college, to travel, to do a year abroad, to reunite with his old friends again. All of this gives me hope.

Because it is purported to take up to six weeks for antipsychotics to take full effect when starting them anew, I figure that it may take that long for them to leave Zach's system completely. But this isn't necessarily the case. It is a complicated scenario. Some of the signs of withdrawal (if you take a more non-medical approach) or relapse (if you adhere to the broken brain perspective) can emerge quickly. Just as there is disagreement about what causes psychosis, so there is disagreement about what happens in the brain when the drugs are curtailed. Those who are not proponents of antipsychotics believe that the dopamine receptors multiply so substantially that the brain is flooded and cannot regulate. Professionals who espouse the bio-medical model suggest that the disease is degenerative, and that the "breakthrough" symptoms are evidence of this.

There are a growing number of mental health professionals, such as Eleanor Longden, Rufus May, and Joanna Moncrieff, who do not consider schizophrenia or psychosis to be diseases, but rather pro-cesses of the body and mind in response to unresolved trauma. I find documentaries and TED Talks on the subject, and I find myself eas-ing into their camp, then questioning my navigation. I feel a bit lost. There are no definitive answers, only more questions.

As part of our dog walking routine, Zach asks me to test his compre-hension and recall of vocabulary.

"I just can't get my words out. Can't you tell? Can't you hear the difference in me?" he says. It is his frustration and agitation that I hear more than anything else. We go through the alpha-bet. I feel myself deliberating, not wanting to patronize him by making the "game" too easy. Neither do I want to stump him by using convoluted vocabulary that could confirm his fear, reinforce his conviction.

"Antiquated. Animosity. Animated. Barricade. Beckoning. Bourgeois."

He does seem to be taking more time than usual to synthesize his thoughts, but it makes sense. He has been through so much. Part of his self, his voice, his core identity has shifted. Whereas on the drugs Zach craved carbohydrates and foraged for food almost all day long, now he has no appetite at all. Instead of sleeping at night, he is wide awake. I am nervous that the psychiatrist will say that it is the affective part of the diagnosis that is rearing its head. For a while I just watch, and I say nothing.

Nance has learned of something called NAMI: the National Alliance for the Mentally Ill. It is a huge network that started from a small, grassroots effort by two mothers who felt that their sons' mental health needs were not being met in the community.

There is a ten-week course called Family-to-Family, run by and for family members like us. "It will educate us," Nance says. I am not sure about it. I am still embarrassed and cloistered. Most of all though, I am shocked that Nance, my normally phlegmatic partner, wants to share our most vulnerable secret.

She mentions it again and again, until I relent. "Okay," I stutter. "I'll go."

She is about to return to San Francisco for another week of work. "I'll call and book us on the next course on my way to the airport," she says, and I see a glint of resolve in her eyes. Then, before she disappears from the bedroom, she smiles, backtracks to me and leans over to kiss me goodbye. Her hair is damp and musky with Argan oil, her lips minty from Burt Bees balm.

"See you on Thursday night," she says. "Have a good day."

Have a good day. Have a good day. I remember all the times gone by that Nance uttered these words before leaving the house. The days really were good back then, more so than I ever realized. They stretched out with work and responsibility and what I considered normality. Good days, when Zach was like his fifteen- or sixteen- or seventeen-year-old peers.

I offer her my cheek, conscious that I haven't brushed my teeth, that I am stale and sweaty from tossing and turning half the night, that she is so very alert and awake and ready to face the day, whereas

I want to go back to sleep, or scream, or hide away. I am not sure if there will ever be good days again. I am worried about Zach's all-or-nothing approach. I am nervous that there is nobody out there leading the way in this experiment that we seem to be embarking upon.

"Somebody in the class might know what we should do," Nance says. "They may have been through this, hon."

"I hope so. I really hope so."

With Nance in Northern California, Dale in Central California and Zach in his own reality that is mostly inaccessible to me, we move further away from the norm of family life. Not that we were ever seen as conventional. Women who were gay, like Nance and I, were classified as mentally ill up until 1973 because of their sexual orientation. In some ways the prejudice is still intense. It is 2009. We are still not allowed to get married in the state of California. There was a window of opportunity in 2008, but it soon closed again. The ban on same-sex marriage will remain until 2011, when Obama will declare it unconstitutional. Nance and I will then tie the knot.

As a young girl I always considered America to be a forward-thinking nation. Yet living here has made me realize more and more how this country is not just homophobic, but also embedded with a structural racism that is shameful beyond measure. This stolen land. The legacy of greed. I know as wretched as our situation is, it could be worse. Black men in this country are much more likely than white men to enter institutions for mental disorders, especially by way of the criminal justice system. It is also this community, often already traumatized after society has failed to acknowledge the pain and suffering they have experienced in their lives, that meet with more compulsorily detention, seclusion and restraint within the psychiatric wards. It seems that so many of our stories are not understood, not heard, that certain groups remain so distinctly out-side of society, and on the margins.

As hard as things are for us all witnessing Zach's pain, it is spring: the fecund season, a constant metaphor for birth, or in our case rebirth. It gets me considering the concept of neuroplasticity, in which the pathways of the brain begin to renew, recalibrate, regen-erate naturally, as if sprouting new shoots. Looking at the calendar, I am aware it will be my birthday soon. Birthdays and Mother's Day used to mean time spent in nature, as a family. It was a tradition, an unwritten rule.

•

The birthday outing that I play, rewind, then play again in my head—like an old tape recorder—is Zach's sixteenth. We chose to visit Santa Catalina Island, the third-largest of the eight California Channel Islands, and the most frequented because of how close it is to Los Angeles.

Once settled in the car, Nance cranked up the CD player to blast out "Mr. Blue Sky" by ELO—our familiar road-trip tune, the one that belonged entirely to us.

> Mr. Blue Sky, please tell us why
> You had to hide away for so long (so long)

The boys beat their thighs with their hands. Nance tapped on the steering wheel. I sang along, making Belle dance on my lap. It was 2005, twenty-one months since mum had died, and a year since we'd lost Auntie. The previous year had been the hardest I'd ever known.

I was comforted by thinking it could never be that bad again, and by knowing the house was mine, as were Nance and the boys. I had so much that I could still cling to.

Unlike the other islands—two of which were controlled by the military and off limits to the public, the other five remaining uninhabited and part of the Channel Islands National Park—Catalina was a haven for tourists. There were hotels, restaurants, water sports and a huge casino in the main town of Avalon. After ferrying across from San Pedro, we rented bikes. Hot from the weather on the island and from riding uphill to the botanical gardens, Nance suggested that we cool off at Crescent Beach. She had never been as much of a fish as the boys and me, but when she did force herself to brave the water, she enjoyed it.

She grabbed my hand like a schoolgirl on a field trip and we tiptoed over the pebbles, jumped the waves. We floated, we frolicked and she swam on my back like a turtle. The boys ventured farther out, bodysurfing. They knew how to read the water like Nance reads a map, like I read a story. They returned to us breathless, hair wet, eyes red from the ocean salt. We gathered in a makeshift circle, treading water. There were surfers and boogie-boarders in our line of vision, but they knew to avoid us, such was the protocol of this territory.

Nance felt it first. I saw her expression change to one of fear. The water rose, and I sensed it too—a whoosh, a slither, a push against my rump. It breached right next to us, and through the spray I saw it. Closer to me than any wild beast had ever ventured, it was gray and colossal: a harbor seal.

Nance and the boys were already making a dash for the shore, but I watched as it turned its heft and looked at me, blinking in the sun. I had touched a marine mammal, or it had touched me, silky smooth, skin to skin.

"How big do you think that animal was? Why did it come so close to us? Could it have hurt us?" I babbled as we got dressed on the sand, my body still pulsing with wild disbelief.

I now had two occasions to fixate upon; one of them at Piedras Blancas and the other on Zach's birthday, both of which had brought me into contact with true seals (known as phocids). Phocids are different from otariids, which are also called sea lions. Otariids have ear-flaps and can turn their large rear flippers around to walk like a dog. Phocids have only ear-holes, and they slither on their stomachs to move on land. There are roughly seventeen to twenty species of phocids, and about the same number again of otariids.

I dreamed of harbor seals after our trip to the island. I was back in the water swimming with them, totally unafraid this time. They slithered onto land with me, where they transformed into sea lions and were able to waddle. When they morphed again, they were human. I was not the first to imagine such a thing. In Norse and Celtic mythology, seal-folk are known as selkies. These legends are mostly set in the Northern Isles of Scotland, but also appear in Faroe-Island tales—habitats closer to my birthplace. Selkies could be either male or female, undergoing a full-body transformation when coming onto land, shedding their skin and becoming fully human. Described as incredibly beautiful, selkies came to land to seek out the dissatisfied, such as the lonely wives of fishermen. They could only remain in the presence of humans for a short period of time before having to return to the sea.

When I woke the next day, the selkies were still on my mind: the tragedy of their entrapment between land and sea, the loss of their skins and the marine world that they were born to, and the sacrifice they made to be with their human family. Selkies knew what it was to fall in love and live for the moment, always with the knowledge that their true place was elsewhere, that this was borrowed time, that one day the world from whence they came would summon them back.

•

It takes a few days after stopping the drugs, but Zach starts eating again. He also resumes smoking weed, or maybe he never really stopped. Nance suggests that we get a testing kit from Rite Aid, and maybe a second kit that detects amphetamine-based drugs, to see if he is taking those as well. It feels like too much to monitor. I am already chauffeuring him to appointments to sign up for benefits, to therapy appointments, to UCLA to meet with the finance office to work out what we need to pay back to the university in grants and loans from the term before last. There is my constant research, too, that is still ongoing, in a bid to understand everything. So the idea of being a pseudo drugs counselor and setting the house up as the local testing center is not appealing in the least. Maybe because my mum never policed me, I don't see the advantage of policing Zach— at least not in this way.

Finally, we are invited to start the NAMI course. As I make my way to the Westside, my stomach aches from the worry of knowing Zach is alone for the evening. I am not sure if it's the weed or the fact he has stopped the antipsychotics and is having withdrawal effects, but he has been forgetting things: leaving the oven on, not being mindful about cleaning up, not locking the front door. Last week Belle got into a pack of Korean ribs from Trader Joe's supermarket that he had left on the coffee table. The salt and spices made her so sick we had to take her to the vet, where she was given charcoal.

"Maybe if he has to tidy up after himself, he will," Nance tells me, and I want to believe her. I hold out from cleaning up after him myself, but when things like the ribs incident happen, it feels so risky.

I tell myself that tonight is a new beginning—another one. Ellyn Saks said we should never give up hope. We are just one year on from the hospital stay. It is still early days, even though there are times when one short orbit around the sun seems to have taken forever.

Nance is flying home from San Francisco just for one night so we can attend this Los Angeles-based course together. Sometimes I miss her during the week; mostly, though, I consider it a mixed blessing being separated by three hundred and fifty miles. Nance doesn't have to live amid all the turmoil and upheaval. Staying with her parents from Monday to Friday, sleeping in the same bedroom that she occupied more than four decades ago, means she can help her mother who is going steadily blind from macular degeneration, and avoid the turmoil and upheaval here at home. It is a different kind of challenge, a blessing to have this time with her folks.

I weave around the parking lot a few times but I cannot see her, so I circumnavigate the block. The neon lettering of the Kirk Douglas Theatre, the streetlights and car headlamps shine in the rain and make me squint.

As I cut back through side streets, between the swish of my windscreen wipers, I see a young man on the pavement, bedding down for the night. He is scruffy, a heap under gray blankets, and muttering to himself, his body just inches from the busy road. I drive on, blink hard and swallow to stem my tears.

I turn back into the parking lot and see Nance getting out of a taxi. "Hon," I shout through the open window, competing with the sound of the rain and my tires on wet asphalt. "You made it."

The meeting takes place in a mental health center—a large white room, chilly in its vastness, with gray floor tiles and matching plastic tables and chairs. The furniture is arranged in the shape of a horse-shoe. We are the last to join the session and a tall older woman with dyed platinum blonde hair and an air of calm confidence waves us to two hard, empty chairs. Her name badge says Laura.

The group members are all middle-aged and tired looking. We have to write our names in black marker on sticky labels and attach them to our chests, as if we might forget who we are. Laura places large ring binders on our tables, and for a moment there is the famil-iar comfort of being in class, being taught, led, spoon-fed by the teacher. Suzie, another facilitator, opens the meeting, reading from the same kind of binder as those distributed to us, only her one is overflowing with information. Her manicured fingers turn the pages and trace the lines as she reads out the history of NAMI and its mis-sion statement.

Suzie is eloquent and slim. She sits with a straight back and a sense of importance. Her sleek auburn hair curls into her thin neck. Between readings she nudges her spectacles down onto the bridge of her nose and peers at us over the rims. She has placed a worn leather briefcase at her feet, which are crossed at the ankle. She is altogether proper.

She asks us to introduce ourselves and the person we are here for. I am still not sure how to open the lid on my voice; I don't know how I will close it again, contain the fear.

Suzie says we don't have to share. We can pass if we want to.

As other people tell their stories, I dig my ragged fingernails into the fleshy heels of my hands to fight the collective feeling of grief in the room. These people have sons, daughters, siblings in their late teens or early twenties. The tales are uncannily similar, and when

Dawn tells us how her son has dropped out of Berkeley after being diagnosed with schizophrenia, I feel Nance shiver.

"Do you want my jacket, honey?" I ask. She shakes her head.

I am most struck by June, a woman who is so fatigued that she crosses her forearms on the table in front of her so she can rest her head upon them. She is hoping to become the legal conservator for her brother, who has been in a board and care home long-term. And Carole, whose son is "free" but sleeps in a dumpster on Santa Monica Boulevard. Carole's sobs are deep and guttural; I feel her pain because it is so akin to my own.

Mum had always said there were people worse off than us in the world. Here, we are the same as every other family in the room. All this sadness—so strangely comforting. In all the chaos, I hadn't realized how isolated I'd become. Suzie, the facilitator, gets to us, and something spurs me on to talk. I give a brief history and tell them that Zach has stopped his antipsychotics, that he has started smoking marijuana again. "I'm not sure what to do," I say.

Nance takes over and explains how we want to learn some ways of coping as a family.

Suzie speaks first. She says I am in the first stage of "mental illness trauma," suffering from denial, shock, hoping against hope. Heads nodding around me show I am not alone.

When the meeting is officially over, some folks stay behind and form a cluster in the parking lot. We close ranks with our backs to the weather. They open their notebooks, unlock their phones and search for contact numbers for consultants, therapists, treatment programs. Some of these people have been living with a family member going through experiences of psychosis for many years. The thought of us being in this situation for the long haul gives me heartburn. I rummage in my bag for an antacid. Nance jots down notes on a piece of paper that rustles in the wind as if trying to escape her. She tucks it into a pocket in the binder, and I watch to make sure it is safe, this little nugget of hope.

8

CRASH

Autumn 2011

Nance's mum, Barb, who is blind and frail, is visiting when Zach asks for money for cigarettes. We refuse. Nance throws him out of the house, tearing his t-shirt. He is indignant, and so is she, and I am once again Piggy in the Middle. This thing I am part of reminds me of my childhood.

Chingford Hall Estate, where roughhousing was common both inside and outside of our home. I don't like it—the memories it kicks up, the drama. I thought I had outgrown violence. Nance is visibly shaken too. For so many years I was the disciplinarian, as Zach's birth mother. Nance took a back seat. But tonight, with her vulnerable mother being jostled, and our property being punched, she was sorely tested.

Zach will hold on to this for years, bringing it up when he is particularly helpless and hopeless, the one and only time that Nance laid hands on him, imprinting on his psyche like a branding iron on the flank of a cow. Instead of going to bed that night, I drive across town to join him in an all-night coffee shop. Caught between the ferocity of my love as a mother and my need, now more than ever, to feel supported by my partner, I feel I am failing them both.

When Barb has returned home and Nance and I are once again alone, we argue. We are in the car on the way back from Home Depot on Sunset Boulevard. It is hot. It starts off petty, about me wanting to ask Zach to help us with the DIY project, and Nance saying she would rather do it alone. We are both so volatile, so emotional. We haven't resolved the incident over Zach and the cigarette money. At Gower and Hollywood, she pounds the dashboard in frustration. I jump out into a busy intersection and try to walk home.

We realize we need help. Nance says she doesn't recognize herself anymore. I am concerned about us both. Nance looks at a list on the Los Angeles lesbian and gay center website. She finds Liza, a local marriage and family therapist based in West Hollywood.

I'm nervous about our first session. Liza's purpose-built studio sits at the back of her garden under a kumquat tree, next to a pond of Koi. She has a kettle and an assortment of tea bags. There is a soft blanket thrown over the back of the couch. I drape it over me, taking care not to put it anywhere near Nance. I know she would worry about who may have last used it to cover up.

Liza writes things down about us on a yellow legal pad, peering over her glasses as if we are models in a life drawing class. It seems she needs to inspect us as well as listen. I let Nance start, but then I fill in.

Our narrative begins with Zach's departure from consensual reality. It is the catalytic event. We open there every time. In medias res. For many months the stage will be set for these sessions, with Zach as the protagonist. Sometimes I want to talk about other things, to ask if our family might be struggling even if Zach had flown the nest, whether we might be putting too much emphasis on the "break" and the fallout. I am defensive. If Nance and Liza agree on a sentiment that I don't, I feel picked on, bullied, ganged up against.

As hard as I try not to, I still field Zach's movements, check his Facebook, phone, bank accounts. It is the statistics—how fifty percent of people with Zach's diagnosis attempt suicide and fifteen percent succeed—that prompt me to hold him close, so close that neither of us can breathe. We are hanging on to each other for dear life.

Both Liza and Nance try to show me that all the vigilance in the world cannot save or fix my boy. He has his own voice. He needs to find it again.

•

It is two years now since Zach's initial diagnosis. Some weeks pass with glimpses of great beauty. Moments I treasure. Dale coming home, the two boys wrestling on the dining room floor. Zach singing while Dale plays guitar. There is more joy when Zach returns part-time to UCLA. On the good days, he attends his college classes.

He is still trying to find ways to help his mood, wake up properly, be the person he felt he used to be. "None of us are who we were, Zigs," I tell him. "Time and experience change us all."

I know this is true, but I also know that being "good" two years ago was vastly different from what it means for him to be "good" now. Being "good" now means being compliant as a patient. It means showing insight into his disease, it means accepting his diagnosis, his "disorder," his "illness"; all the reductive language used to describe him; the drugs, the doctors, the treatments, the therapies.

Being "good" means growing into his identity as a "sick" person. It means me embracing that identity, accepting it too. I hear myself say the words on the phone, in appointments, to claim benefits, to deal with health insurance. *My son has a mental illness, a serious mental illness, an enduring mental illness. My son has psychosis NOS, schizoaffective disorder, paranoid schizophrenia.* It still sounds so wrong to my ears, disabling. But I don't know how to catapult us out of this net we are caught in without landing us back in the sea, out of our depth and treading water. I will though. I will learn.

Zach makes an appointment with yet another new psychiatrist and requests an assessment for ADD and a prescription for Adderall, an amphetamine-based drug that students often sell to each other at parties, or when exams and assignments are due. Adderall makes it easy to pull all-nighters. It is the Friday before finals week. Zach says he is going to study. He takes the Adderall to help him focus. Antipsychotics are so sedating, and Zach has had to start them again, a few times now, mostly at my insistence, or that of his doctors, after the abrupt withdrawal of the drugs left him in a state of distress. He wants to be awake, to partake of life. He feels Adderall helps him to do so.

At 11 p.m. a police officer calls me. Zach has been in a car accident and is being admitted to Ronald Regan UCLA Medical Center. He can't give me any more information. Once more, I race toward the emergency room. Veteran Avenue is blocked off.

I see flares, a car flipped on its roof and Zach's vehicle, the driver's side T-boned, being towed away. I can't imagine anyone surviving an accident of this magnitude. All I can think about is the Adderall, and that fucking idiot psychiatrist. My son. He could be dead or paralyzed.

I park haphazardly in an area where I could get a fine, get towed away, and I run from the car. Inside, I tell the receptionist who I am, why I am here.

"Is he okay? Is he alive?" She is checking the computer. Every second counts. I peer through the locked door to the ER.

I see him just inside, lying on a gurney on a carrying board, wearing a neck collar. Reception buzzes me in. "Oh my god. Move your fingers and toes," I scream. He does. I want to slap him and hug him at the same time.

A doctor reassures me that both drivers suffered only whiplash, and that they are extremely lucky. An x-ray is recommended because of the impact and the stress to Zach's neck. But he is impatient, and signs a form to discharge himself. He is released, shaken but hungry. He wants to know whether In-N-Out Burger is still open.

"How can you eat? Aren't you in shock?" I ask.

"Yes, I think I am. I need sugar for it," he says, rubbing his neck.

My head throbs. My innards feel wrung out like an old dish-cloth. There is a parking attendant by my car. He is taking down my registration plate, a perplexed look on his face as he realizes the vehicle is unlocked, the driver side door ajar.

"Sorry," I say. "My son was in an accident." He nods and says something about how thankful I should be that I didn't get a ticket, but I am stuck in fight or flight, feeling palpitations rather than gratitude.

Zach saunters to the vehicle, as if he is on holiday. "Get in," I say. It's a wonder I didn't crash my own car. I could have lost him, despite all my tracking and checking and following. He could have died. I am angry and relieved and exhausted.

At the intersection of Westwood Boulevard and Wilshire, I pose the question I have held on to until now. "Did you take more than one pill? The Adderall?"

"Yes, just one more, but it made my judgment better. My reflexes are faster on it. I'm telling you, it wasn't my fault."

"That's what you think. That's your perception."

"Why doesn't anyone believe me?" he asks.

I want to tell him why in no uncertain terms, but then, luckily, Dale calls.

Home for the weekend but staying with friends, Dale has made his way to Westwood after speaking to Nance. We convene at the fast-food joint. I haven't seen my eldest son look so drawn and tired in ages. It plagues me. When I run in to use the bathroom and look at myself in the mirror, I have the same pallor and tired, empty stare.

The next morning, Zach's neck hurts, but he still doesn't want to have an x-ray. I decide to drive back with Dale to Santa Barbara and spend a rare day alone with him. Before we pull the door shut behind us, I hear Zach telling Nance that it wasn't his fault. He was trying to do a U-turn when a car that was speeding hit him. She starts to explain the rules of the road to him. I decide not to get involved anymore, to let the police and the insurance company make the final verdict. I want to be present for Dale today, to try to show him he is important too.

"Let's rent bikes, and eat tacos, and go whale-watching," I suggest.

I know that my first-born has inherited a legacy of guilt and responsibility, because of Zach's situation. He isn't alone in this respect either. Other young men and women in his position often feel like the forgotten family members. Their brother or sister with the diagnosis have more important problems than they do.

I have spoken to the NAMI mothers about this, and they have told me how their "well" children have a fear that they might catch or develop the same diagnosis as their sibling with the extreme mental distress. Along with this, there is a sense of survivor's guilt. Statistics show that the "well" siblings are also twice as likely to experience low mood compared with the rest of the population.

———————

Dale offers to drive. He takes the wheel with one hand, the seat pushed way back to make room for his long legs. I feel a swell of emotion as I notice him without my normal sense of distraction: his angular jaw and freckled nose. We take the 101 northbound, where the landscape grows more mountainous and wild. Something about the wide, fast road makes me brave, so I blurt out, "I'm sorry about how much you've been eclipsed by Zach's difficulties, how I was too preoccupied to see it."

Dale is quiet. He takes time to talk. He doesn't have my degree of impulsivity. It is a trait that serves him well where Zach is concerned. He listens to his brother, understands without having had any formal training.

"It's okay," he says, "I get it. I'm an adult now."

We pass Cabrillo, the spot where Dale likes to surf. I face the rugged shoreline, the huge blue canvas of the Pacific. Palm trees line the sand. Pelicans weave in and out of their flight pattern then dive bomb for fish, but this is not what I am thinking about. In my mind's eye, I picture the future. I see the boys without me in the frame.

I would like to voice my fear of what will happen to Zach when I am no longer around, to air these pressing questions that we have both skirted around so far, when Dale, with all the intuition of an empath, says, "It's okay mum. After last night I know that I won't be able to replace you. I can't be Zach's primary caregiver. It would be too much of a strain on me."

"I understand," I say, thankful for his honesty.

"I'll do what I can," Dale says. He sighs. He sighs a lot—big, audible, deep sighs that have their own pitch of sorrow.

Dale pulls up at the bike rental shop on the promenade. We rent two beach cruisers and ride side by side down to the pier.

"Look," he points. I follow his index finger. Out at sea, arcs of foam and spray spout into the air. "I think they're humpbacks on their way to Mexico."

I stop the bike, place my feet on the ground. Dale does the same. We stand watching this miraculous sight together, the two of us. So far from where we began our life as mother and son. When the whales stop breaching and spouting, I smile and squeeze Dale's bicep.

"Wow," we both say.

Dale has a better color today. His eyes glint in the sun as he surveys the surf.

"I might get my board out later," he tells me.

"I'm glad you have the water, D. Please be careful."

The week after the accident, Nance can't get back to Los Angeles, so I go to therapy alone. I tell Liza about it all—the Adderall, the crash. She asks me to consider my worst fear: Zach dying before me. I weep all the way home. When I go to sleep, I dream I am searching for him, following the beeps of his computer game, running from room to room, calling his name.

9

AÑO NUEVO

Winter 2014

I t happens steadily, but when I stop to take stock, I realize some things have changed—for the better. Zach, now twenty-four, has stopped waking me up in the night so much. He seems less scared, less lonely. He resists taking so many showers in the early hours, which I later find out is his way of drowning out the more difficult voices. He doesn't raid the fridge as frequently during the night. In fact, his nocturnal default is gradually changing to diurnal. He moves differently, more freely. He has started to shave and brush his teeth regularly again.

"Now don't get your hopes up too much, Tan," Nance says.

"No, of course not," I reply, but I am already sending up little prayers of gratitude to the God I had given up on.

I am busily distracted these days, which is useful. We have decided to put the upper, fully contained floor of our home on Airbnb to get some extra cash to help pay our overheads. I shop for breakfast provisions, change sheets, polish the hardwood floor, greet guests and tell them the story of the house. I have responsibility and structure in my day.

Zach rises to new challenges too. He re-enrolls at UCLA. This time he signs up with the Extension College. He has stopped and started his studies so many times now at the main campus that in order to continue to receive funding he needs to pay for and get a passing C grade in at least one class. As well as his studies, he offers to be a subject for a research project, using physical exercise and computer games to try to improve cognition. The department provides him with a tablet to electronically record the amount and type of exercise he does each day. There are targets he needs to reach. The computer games measure his reflexes, his memory and cognitive response.

"I like it," he says, bustling into the kitchen, where I am cooking. He shows me the results of his first week of cardio in a graph on the screen.

I like it too. I see him waking up, getting the bus to Westwood and partaking in the program willingly. He seems altogether softer and kinder.

I know that now he is feeling more autonomous, he wants to find someone to share a deeper and more meaningful relationship with. Girlfriends have been an important part of Zach's life and identity from such an early age, and he never had much trouble finding them throughout high school and his first year of college. Being in his early twenties and struggling to understand what happened to him (and why) creates loneliness—so does the label, the system, the separation from the mainstream. A girlfriend would be an affirmation, a validation. Zach craves both.

Alongside being a student, and a subject in the research study for UCLA, Zach enrolls in a county-run supported employment program, where he works in the kitchen chopping vegetables and cooking for homeless people. I drop him off and pick him up when I am able, when I don't have too much else going on.

One afternoon, when he has finished a shift, he leaves work with Carlos, a Guatemalan by birth, who has a diagnosis of schizophrenia. They become fast friends, confiding in each other and surfing on their days off. Carlos tells Zach about a psychiatrist he consulted who prescribes orthomolecular medicine.

Orthomolecular treatment uses a natural protocol of vitamins and supplements in high doses. American chemist Linus Pauling coined the term "orthomolecular" in the 1960s to mean "the right molecules in the right amounts" (the Greek *ortho* implies "correct"). Proponents of orthomolecular medicine hold that treatment must be based on each patient's individual biochemistry. It is still a scientific model, but not a one-size-fits-all ideology.

Although Orthomolecular doctors are few and far between, we find one who practices this form of medicine in the city of Santa Barbara. He has patented a supplement called ProFrontal, which he believes supports the NMDA receptor in the brain (NMDA is thought to play a critical role in cognitive and psychological functions). We order some of the supplement online. It is made from sarcosine and N-acetyl cysteine. The sarcosine contains sulfur and smells like a combination of bad eggs and burnt matches, but Zach is willing to try it. I want to get an appointment with this doctor for Zach, but he is booked up for months in advance.

Without the privilege of an individual consultation, we refer to a list of vitamins and minerals that Carlos's doctor had prescribed for him, and order a bulk supply of everything on it. The niacin makes Zach's face flush a beetroot red, which it is supposed to do, and the ProFrontal seems to help his focus. The regime includes vitamin B, vitamin D, zinc, magnesium and a dose of fish oils. I help Zach measure out the dosages and feel hope rising inside me.

We are in the living room, hanging out with Belle, when he tells me how he feels.

His words are so encouraging, I want to capture them and put them in a pendant around my neck, or in a purse of red velvet that I can hold on to forever.

"I feel really warm, and just more present. I am more here," he says, pointing to his forehead. I hug him. I kiss him on the spot that he has singled out. I make a note to order some more, maybe a job lot, and to write a testimonial for the site and tell everyone I know in the world, in case they need it or know anyone who needs it or may need it in the future.

A few weeks in, and Zach claims that the supplements have been out of his sight, and possibly meddled with. Unless he can order them all individually foil-wrapped and pick them up daily from a compound pharmacy, he is not willing to continue with them. This is not feasible. These drugs are not pharmaceutically made. I try to plead with him, help him to see reason.

"You can keep them in your room, in your backpack, on your person even?" But his mind is made up, and my dear son, who even before had all the makings of a stubborn Scorpio, cannot be persuaded otherwise. It is proof that Nance is right, I mustn't get my hopes up. We are always just inching forward incrementally in this dance of emergence, and progress—however it is measured—can be shot down in an instant.

Carlos's mum is a champion of alternative remedies and a clean vegan diet. She refers us to an integrative doctor in Culver City who has expertise in pharmacogenetic testing and believes that psychosis is caused by brain inflammation. Zach is prescribed antibiotics. For a while his mood seems less low, but he wants an MRI of his brain to see if anything shows up. It doesn't.

This integrative psychiatrist tests Zach's saliva and the results show a double mutation of MTHFR (methylenetetrahydrofolate reductase) a genotype that, according to this psychiatrist's beliefs, places Zach at slightly higher odds of developing psychosis. This means that both Gordon and I carry the mutation; that it is our fault in one sense after all—if you believe in functional medicine, that is.

Zach is given methylfolate supplement. The doctor suggests that I take the supplement too. Conventional medicine sees functional medicine as quackery, but nothing about the broken-brain model has worked for us so far. Whether or not this kind of testing is reliable, I do not know, but the treatment is gentler. There is a tangibility about it that I want to grasp on to. I have a mutation, one with thirteen syllables. I am more like Zach than unlike him now, and I take the same pill that turns my urine a vibrant yellow to prove it.

I know there is much that Zach doesn't tell me, fearful of my reactions, scared that it may lead to him going into the hospital again. On some days we fast, we juice, we try all kinds of things. We sometimes grow impatient and disillusioned.

Carolyn, our acupuncturist, visits and sages the house in case we have attracted spirits. She calls them playful, but we know this isn't a game. She reminds Zach to pray to the archangels of light—Gabriel, Michael, Raphael and Uriel. Zach gets down on his knees to ask the angels to drown out the noise in his head. I pray too, on all fours on the dusty hardwood floor. I pray that Zach will continue to get better, and that he will be able to manage like Ellyn Saks and Carlos. I emphasize the word manage, because it is positive, unlike the other words that have been used to define Zach in the past. I have been told by professionals that schizoaffective disorder, or psychosis, cannot be cured, but is instead managed. I hate the former language, with all its references to disorders and illnesses and conditions, but the idea of managing is fine. I welcome managing. Nance is a manager. We all want to manage our own lives.

As the summer of 2015 comes to an end, Zach tells us he wants to try living alone, separating, and relying on peers and professionals rather than us. It is a sign of maturity and independence, one I thought might not be possible just a couple of years ago.

Homes for Life is a housing project that is being built in the San

Fernando Valley. It will predominantly serve the homeless, but three of the units are going to be reserved for residents who are said to be experiencing extreme mental and emotional states. It is difficult to find supported housing that is subsidized by government assistance housing projects. We know how fortunate we are. Zach will have his own bedroom, kitchen, living room and bathroom on the third floor of an apartment block with a laundry room, a rooftop garden and a community room. A support worker will be available during daytime hours and a manager five nights a week. His apartment comes with everything, including a television.

To make his home complete, he rescues a part-Bengal cat from the local animal shelter and calls him Richard Parker. The name is not lost on us. Richard Parker is the Bengal tiger that weathers the storm with the human protagonist Piscine in *The Life of Pi*. It is unclear whether the tiger exists, or is a figment of Pi's imagination, a representation of the good Lord. But whoever he is, he helps Pi survive.

Zach moves in, and together we fill his cupboards and fridge with food. He may truly have a home for life, or at least for as long as he wants it. Stable housing is so crucial for everyone.

"My son is doing well," I tell everyone. It is true. He is.

He starts to look more seriously for a girlfriend, and connects with a girl called Savanna on Tinder. She is a college graduate interning in the music industry in Los Angeles. Her family is of Romanichal Gypsy origin. Settled in Texas, they have an enormous trailer that they live in for part of the year, and an even more enormous extended family. Zach pulls up outside our house one night and shyly introduces us to her. I take to her quickly. She is dressed in a top that she made herself, cutting the fabric into strips to reveal her shoulders. She has applied her make-up with expertise. Eyelashes that curl up to the sky and shades of pink and mauve on her lids that look like a moody sunset. She is free-spirited and open, and I am excited that Zach has found someone who has a heart full of passion and adventure.

It is still early in their relationship when we all go camping on the Monterey coast. While Dale and Zach wrestle on the sand, and Nance sets up camp, Savanna and I trail the water's edge. She asks me about Zach—the things he has told her about his experiences, but not elaborated upon. I don't want to scare her, but I also don't want to deceive her. It is Zach's place to tell, and perhaps, with the miracle of love and companionship, he might bloom and flourish. I believe that there is someone for everyone, and a relationship might truly help to heal his pain. The past should not dictate the future. I want to support the gift they have uncovered together. Savanna is younger than Zach, just twenty-one to his twenty-five.

We worry when Zach leaves Homes for Life just a few months later. We had all worked so hard, and against all odds, to secure a place for him, but he wants to live with Savanna. They want to live with each other. Savanna finds a small place for them both in West Hollywood, a happening part of town just steps away from cool restaurants and vintage shops, and the famous Old Hollywood Farmers' Market.

They move in together in the early autumn of 2016, and he starts to smile again, sporting hip clothes, grooming himself and taking Savanna out to eat. She advises him on what to wear and cuts his hair. He serenades her on the guitar. They look bright-eyed and happy together, the way two people look when they are young and flooded with oxytocin—the love hormone—and the promise of togetherness.

Nance and I have spent months thinking about moving to Northern California, so we can be close to San Francisco where Nance's office is based, where Nance's mum Barb—now ailing—lives, and where, just like the song suggests, I have left my heart. It is greener, cooler, more like England in the Bay Area. With Zach being so dependent on me, and me being so entangled, so ready to make everything better, there hasn't been the opportunity to up and relocate, but now seems like a time to try; to turn to Nance, to let Zach be free to live his life while I try to navigate my own.

On the weekends I go north to join Nance instead of her coming home to Los Angeles. We drive around the countryside south of San Francisco, looking at parcels of land where we could build a tiny house. We know that building off-grid is fraught with bureaucracy, but it doesn't stop us pointing at the mountain homes dotted high above the Lexington Reservoir on Highway 17 and imagining a different life.

"Backing up against a vineyard or a state park would be best," Nance says. "We wouldn't have homes being built right on top of us that way."

I see the listing on Craigslist—a 450-square-foot redwood cabin for rent in the Santa Cruz Mountains. We think that renting, at least initially while we get our bearings, might be more suitable for us.

Nance goes to view the place during her lunch break, and video calls me excitedly on her way back down the mountain. She waves the phone out of the window so I can see the densely forested surroundings and the winding road that leads from the property down to the main road.

"You'll love it, Tan, and it's just twenty minutes from my office."

"The road looks so dangerous," I say, wondering if I will honestly be able to summon the courage to drive up and down it.

"You'll be fine," she tells me. "Just take it slow. Nights will be easier because you'll see the headlights of the other cars. And to be honest, I don't think there'll be much traffic. There are very few homes up here. It's such a find. You'll like the owners. Simon is a science writer and Kathleen is an artist. I think we should snap it up."

I fly up the next day to see the cabin for myself. It is beautifully built, the high ceiling makes it deceptively spacious, and the sleeping area is up in the loft. It is partially furnished. The cabin was originally built in 1850 for the loggers who stayed in the forest up here. The current owners, both retirees from the tech industry, bought the twenty-acre property as part of a ten-year plan. Alongside the cabin and another outbuilding that they renovated, they built their own home on the land.

Named Lakeview Bird Farm, it's home to a menagerie of rescued animals: a llama called Dakota, two alpacas, Frank and Omer, four Channel Island goats, who for some reason are all named Mary, four dogs, twice as many cats, an emu called Sassy, a henhouse full of chickens and a rooster called Lucky.

Simon leads us across a suspension bridge to the treehouse he built; it makes me feel intrepid. "I like it," I tell Nance. Before we leave, I give Omer some grain from a huge steel bin, laughing at the way he chews and shows us his long yellow teeth. I think about what it would be like to live here, to sleep in a loft in a cabin in the mountains. As a little girl my favorite storybook was *Heidi*. She slept in a loft on a bale of hay at her grandfather's cabin in the Swiss Alps.

"It's yours if you want it," Kathleen explains.

"I want it," I tell Nance, feeling excitement warm my middle. We sign a one-year lease and Nance writes a check for the deposit.

"I think it's the right thing to rent given our responsibilities back in Los Angeles," I say, as we make our way to the airport. "This way we can see how we cope with mountain life."

I tell Zach and Savanna I will only be five hours away by car, or fifty minutes by plane if they need me, which is nothing by the American scale of travel and distance. I know I will be back and forth a fair bit because of our Los Angeles home, which we continue to run as an Airbnb. I employ a cleaner, a gardener, someone to put the bins out on a Thursday night and bring them in again on a Friday morning, and I stock the home with everything needed for the guests. I am still responsible for oversight as a Superhost, a title bestowed upon me by the Airbnb community for doing such a good job. I cling to the affirmation—the praise for something I have done well.

Bit by bit we move our things from our Los Angeles property to our tiny sanctuary in the mountains.

"It doesn't have to be permanent," Nance reminds me, when the change feels too drastic and I worry about being so far away from Los Angeles and Zach. "Let's see how it goes. We can change our minds anytime."

With this proviso, I turn to our new existence. My neighborhood walks are idyllic, up to the open space at the top of the mountain, past stables, vineyards and multimillion-dollar mansions set back from the road.

I miss Zach, though, and check my phone constantly. The reception isn't ideal in the mountains. He doesn't talk to me as much now that he has Savanna in his life, which I try to interpret as a good sign. He is turning to his partner to meet his needs rather than me. It is time to shed the last layers of everything I have held onto.

Northern California, although just 350 miles north of Los Angeles, has seasons that are more definable, and that in time we will experience. The rainy season, when trees will be uprooted and block the mountain road. Fire season, which after a long, hot, dry summer will cause us much hypervigilance.

I push myself to forge a new identity, to move from the hurried pace of our old routine in Los Angeles into the slow nights of autumn under the redwoods, of homemade soup and mulled wine, and wood fires that Nance builds and stokes when she comes home from work.

There is a NAMI group in nearby San Jose, where I meet some mothers who walk along the Los Gatos Creek trail once a week. They invite me to join them, and just like my NAMI mothers down south, they soon become kin, extending my ever-growing family, understanding my battle scars because they wear the same wounds. Talking and walking in nature will always be my medicine. It is because of this, although I don't know it yet, that a tiny seed of an idea starts germinating slowly in the darkest part of me, searching for the sunlight.

•

My preoccupation with northern elephant seals resurfaces. Mirounga angustirostris—the species that inhabit the Pacific Northwest coast, are distinct from Mirounga leonina, the southern elephant seals that inhabit Argentina and the Galapagos Islands. These extreme divers, swimmers and battling pinnipeds have lain as dormant in my mind as a spruce in winter. But shortly after we move into the cabin, with a little digging around online, I find Año Nuevo, an elephant-seal breeding ground since the 1950s. It lies just forty-five minutes southwest of Los Gatos by car.

As well as being a local surf spot for those skilled enough to navigate the rocks, Año (as the resident rangers, docents and scientists refer to the state park) is also a sanctuary for a notably high number of coastal birds, some of them listed as federally endangered. It sits farther away from the road than the Central Coast rookery in Piedras Blancas, where I first set eyes on the elephant seals, but it is more accessible than San Miguel, the most northerly Channel Island, which has the largest sea-lion and elephant-seal rookery in the world. The main points where the seals can be viewed are reached only by a three mile out-and-back hike over sand dunes. Visitors must book their guided tours in advance online.

When my friend, Debs, from England—whom I haven't seen in a decade—arranges to come out and visit us, she tells me she likes to walk in nature.

"Bring some sturdy walking shoes that are good for getting over sand dunes," I tell her, excited and curious about the adventure ahead of us. "I want to take you somewhere special."

We journey out to the park within days of Debs arriving. Tourists come from all over the world to drive this stretch of coastline on bicycles and motorcycles, in sports cars with soft-tops, in camper vans and trailers. It is an iconic highway, rugged and windswept, and dotted with state beach campsites along the way. I have traveled on the California 1 Highway North when we went the long way to Nance's childhood home. We came inland at Santa Cruz, though, so I have never ventured along this particular part of the coast before. We blast the radio in my Toyota Prius and sing along to the Beach Boys. Debs makes me turn off the road at every scenic overlook along the way so she can snap pictures and post them on Facebook.

When the battery starts to deplete on her phone and she has taken more photos than David Bailey, we edge into Año Nuevo. Along with the hot ocean breeze, the view literally steals our breath away. It is the Galapagos Islands of California, the Serengeti of the sea, teeming with wildlife, both protected and endangered. It is home to coyotes, bobcats, mountain lions, San Francisco red garter snakes and tree frogs, and, of course, the magnificent elephant seals.

On our way out to view the seals, we venture down to Cove Beach to watch the ocean crash onto the rocky shore. I stare down at the shells right in front of me, and up at Debs's hair flapping around her face. Brown pelicans squawk and dive into the water, and I feel what I can only presume is happiness, completeness, a sense of gratitude. If there is anywhere in the world that I want to return to, it is here, with Nance, Zach and Dale.

Farther out, at the viewing platform at South Point, there are elephant seals galore on the sand. They make little grunting noises that sound like a cross between a fart and a trumpet. A docent stands to attention in her red uniform, armed with charts and visual materials about the animals and their behavior.

Debs borrows a pair of binoculars from the docent to observe the giant marine mammals, while I test the docent's skinny on the subject, firing off a list of questions.

"How old are they? What sex are they? Do they come back here every time after their migration? How much do they weigh? What are their predators here? What do they eat? Why does that little one over there look scabby?"

She really knows her stuff, this woman in the red jacket. There is a sense of great passion for her subject too. She has been doing this for more than ten years, and it shows in her weathered skin, her stance as she braces the elements, her recall of facts and stories. She doesn't even need the props but she shares them with us anyway. Photographs and statistics.

"There is a course for members of the public who are interested in training to become docents," she tells me. "It's one of the most esteemed programs in the state of California."

As we journey back to the park entrance, Debs appropriates my phone to take yet more photographs.

"You would be so good at that docent thing," she remarks.

"Really?" I say, thinking about how I am a city girl by birth, how I have lived my whole life in an urban setting, how I know nothing about marine biology. I cast my mind back to our trips to Southend-on-Mud, to the ignorance with which I used to throw candy wrappers out of the car window, grind cigarette butts into the pavement under my heels, go to zoos and circuses. I had no sense of the preservation of the environment. How could I be a tour guide with such a guilty past? Also, I would be doing it for selfish reasons. It would all be for me, to try to take my mind off Zach.

"You *should* do something just for yourself," Debs insists, framing a shot of Año Nuevo Island from the top of the sand dunes. She knows how hard the last few years have been. In some ways, I feel like everyone can see the accumulated stress in my posture and my tired complexion, in my mouth that turns down now at the corners if it is left to its own natural state of being.

Uncannily enough, though, it is not these qualms of not knowing enough about nature and the environment that concern me, nor do they stop me from applying to do the training. The nagging anxiety that still haunts me is to do with something else. It happens at night when the sun goes down over the Santa Cruz Mountains, when the valley turns from a tie-dye pink and purple to a deep velvet blue, when the very last of the diablo wind blows hot and dry through the window of the loft before winter takes hold completely.

The fear hides out in me in a way that defies words. It is all feeling. I am prey to it, waiting, as if a cougar might pounce on my back. I am afraid that I have made a rash move, I am afraid of being three hundred and fifty miles from Los Angeles. I am afraid that I shouldn't be here at all, at the cabin, at Año, or anywhere so far away from Zach. I am afraid to tell Nance. I am afraid to tell anyone. I am just afraid.

10

STRANDED

Somehow, I have managed to pass my training. With the help of a mentor called Kelly—who has been unfailingly patient, even when I asked the same questions again and again—I am now qualified to take people out on my own. I have a manual full of facts which is too heavy to cart with me on the tours, but I have synthesized the main findings and I keep the notes on index cards, together with some photographs that I use as props.

I turn to my docent life, my other identity. I am on an early shift today. I pin my name badge onto the lapel of my red jacket. It says *Tanya Frank: Docent Naturalist*. The uniform helps to disguise me, to make me look authentic. Most of my fellow docents are retired from their day jobs. They seem to have a handle on everything at home. They give up precious time to interpret and translate the behavior of elephant seals, to make the findings fresh and interesting to others. They look confident and generous, or at least that is my impression.

I say goodbye to Nance, and she smiles at me. She has been rooting for me during my training, proud of me each time I leave the safety of the cabin and my preoccupation with Zach, to venture south into the wilds of the park for my lessons. I don't confess that he is still on my mind, that I can't shake him loose, that I feel like a fraud for accepting her praise.

I ease my way down the steep terrain of Montevina Road, staying in a low gear. I slow for Simon, the property owner, and his friends out on their morning walk. They congratulate me too, as if I am doing something good for the planet, as if my environmental consciousness is at the forefront of my work, not my need to survive as a person in my own right. They don't know I need something I can talk about with Nance other than Zach, something that doesn't make her sigh, or her eyes glaze over with burnout.

I take the Pacific Coast Highway, passing kelp-strewn beaches, farm shops selling pies and fresh jams. More than a year has passed since we signed the lease. I am not scared of driving up and down our mountain road anymore, and I can fearlessly navigate Highway 17, the tight bends and steep grades that cut through the coastal mountain range, making it one of the most dangerous roads in the country.

Crossing the bridge at Waddell Creek, I see the point of Año Nuevo jutting out into the Pacific. Beyond the skinny finger of land lies the island, wild and windswept and off limits to the public.

Turning off the highway toward the park, I am careful to heed the 10-mph speed limit. There are a lot of cars ahead of me this morning.

I must wait. For someone who is perpetually late, I also suffer from an ironic degree of impatience. I think I inherited it from my mother. As I creep slowly forward, I contemplate the idea of time, how it passes, how I have spent so much of it wishing for Zach to find peace, lamenting that he might not, waiting for a new answer, a new doctor, a new drug, a new accommodation, a new insurance, a new improvement that might just suddenly happen because I'd read it could.

These days, I wait to see if Zach might be able to complete his studies, regain some of his lost cognitive function, live without stopping and starting the heavy-duty drugs he so despises, find some equilibrium.

This is what I hang on to, this is what I wait for, and somehow in the realm of the elephant-seal sanctuary it seems like it might be possible. It is the closest I can get to believing in miracles on the one hand, and moving toward acceptance on the other.

One of the park interpreters pokes his head out of the kiosk window and hands me the clipboard so I can sign in for my duty. He looks tired and irritable.

"We have a seal that's gone walkabout," he says, pulling a face. "A juvenile bull, made it over the dunes and onto the trail just north of Cove Beach."

I reckon that Cove Beach is at least two miles from where the elephant seals have hauled out this season. I also know that this bull won't have eaten since arriving here two months ago, and that as an adolescent he is too young to mate, so it is not reproductive instinct that explains his wandering. The elephant seals conserve their energy in the same way my mum used to save the electricity: vigilantly. On an especially hot day they may take a dip in the water or engage in a short-lived mock battle if they are young and male, but they do not traverse far from the breeding ground. The alphas move more, fighting to win dominance and protect their harems, but the rest of the animals stay still, especially the pregnant and nursing females, as they wait until it is time to haul out for their long migration.

"It's like Bedlam out there. We've had to turn all the tours around that aren't pre-booked," the interpreter says, his brows knitting with worry.

I expect him to radio through to the roost with news of my arrival, because it is all about logistics from here on out. Twenty minutes of fast walking will get me to the staging area with enough time to spare before the guests trek out for their tour of the park. With so many hundreds of guests being chaperoned daily through the park, it is all a finely choreographed dance. But today, like the elephant seal bull, the interpreter is distracted.

"You'll see all the commotion," he tells me, looking anxiously over my shoulder at the school buses heading his way. "The rangers have called Patrick out to try and help them."

Patrick is the head of the marine mammal science department at the University of California, Santa Cruz, which makes him the de facto director of the reserve. He is regularly spotted here supervising research students on the beach. I rush to park my car, filled with both apprehension and curiosity about the young male that has lost his way and is causing such disarray at the park.

My walk starts along the main trail that leads to Cove Beach. The sea sparkles on mornings like this, a shimmer of deep blue-green with frothy caps. As the waves ebb, I can see the rocks that are normally submerged. There are fault lines running through these parts, creating volatile undercurrents and high swell for the surfers. They are out in force this morning in their black rubbery wetsuits, walking on water.

I pick up my pace at the curved wooden bridge over the inlet. The sun is rising above the old creamery and the horse barn. In the distance I can make out the rangers in khaki, and the docents in red. There is quite a gathering by the time I reach the scene. The elephant-seal bull is lying on the gravel path. It is odd to see him here. He should be basking on the dunes or mock-fighting in the shallows with another male juvenile. As I get closer, I see his proboscis, one of the tell-tale measures of his age. He must be about five or six years old. I can confirm he is male as, aside from his larger body and trunk-like nose, I can see his penile opening just below the dark shadow scar of his umbilicus. The female elephant seal has a shorter nose, and her genitalia is closer to her anus.

It is warm at the park today, even by the water. The seal's breathing is so labored it is audible. Instinctively, he raises a flipper, and digs his digits into the ground to try to scoop up sand and shower it over his body to cool himself. But there is no beach here, just stones and willow. He is in unfamiliar terrain. I feel sorry for this mighty animal who has clearly lost his way. He has begun his catastrophic molt, leaving parts of his skin scaly and dry, and other parts new and smooth.

I look into his eyes. They are not black and shiny like those of a seal pup, nor are they old and milky like those of a sea turtle, but something in between—startled and searching and fixed on the horizon.

I am within striking distance if he decides to flip his tail or fins. Normally we are asked to remain at least twenty-five feet from the seals in case they decide to fight and we inadvertently get trampled, but also because this is their home, their sanctuary—at least that is what it's meant to be. The seals have right of way here, and if they get too close to the trails designated for the tours, the rangers reroute us, using ropes and signs and walkie-talkies. It is a legal requirement of the sanctuary to give the creatures space to exist in their natural habitat without human intrusion.

Sometimes I wonder, though, about this definition. We are here. The footprint is evident, even though all our trash gets carried back out, and nobody (aside from a select few scientists) is allowed to go down onto the beach to disturb the animals. There is a lot of human traffic. As well as the many guests that trundle through this unspoiled landscape clicking cameras, their kids pushing, shoving and shouting with amusement, there are also the scientists, like Patrick and his students, who are out early before the tours start, privately weighing and measuring the animals, doing blood draws, attaching tracking instruments to their heads or flippers, or anesthetizing them if the experiment demands it. These animals, whose lives are mysterious in so many ways, and whom we know so little about in the overall scheme of things, are fascinating to us. Año is built upon our curiosity and fear. So I am torn. On one hand I want to know everything. On the other, I wonder why we can't leave them the fuck alone.

As I bear witness to the plight of this wandering male teenage elephant seal, remaining closer to him than I have been to any elephant seal to date, I am moved by the sheer privilege of being let into this inner circle of observers, especially because, unlike Patrick and the other docents, this is only my first season, my fifth or sixth walk. Generally, these monstrous seals do not charge like buffalo or sneak up and attack like mountain lions—their docility was what almost wiped them out, not just once, not twice, but three times in the past. This history, the number of staff and the rules of the park give me a semblance of security. But I fear this seal, like the elements, might go rogue. Just as I can't control a tsunami, I don't have power over a colossal marine mammal. These beasts can move at a speed of five miles per hour on sand. Maybe as human beings we *like* to feel threatened, just the tiniest bit, because when Patrick asks us to remain alert and step back a few feet, to be ready to run if we need to, we look at each other with wide, intense eyes.

Patrick tells us that this is the furthest he has ever known a seal to wander from the rest of the group at the colony. He has no idea what may have motivated the adolescent to stray, or what might entice him to return. It isn't as if Patrick can waggle a tasty fish or squid in front of his nose to encourage this big guy to move. His fast is absolute—not like my own dietary fads, where a hunger pang or a slight temporary weakness has me foraging in the fridge for sustenance.

Patrick is stumped, despite his scientific know-how, but he improvises like a stand-up comedian on stage, like a clown at the circus. He takes one strong arm, raises it above his head and bends it at the wrist, making a pseudo-elephant trunk. He then calls the young seal, with a throaty bellowing noise like a motorbike engine, and causes us, the audience, to laugh. The seal lumbers forward, and his colossal frame, that must weigh in at about 1,100 kilos, makes the ground shake.

A message comes through on the radio from the roost, asking for docents to make their way to the staging area for the tours. As we assemble for duty, the volunteer coordinator, Christen, is worried. "That seal could have a heart attack," she says, "and we have to act as if everything is fine." I realize with horror that the show must go on, that we must pretend we are in control and know what we are doing. We are told we mustn't mention the bull that has strayed and is stranded miles from home.

"Tanya, can you take the next school group?" Christen asks me.

"I haven't had the school-group training," I tell her, now doubly concerned about how I will rein in a potentially undisciplined class of fourth-graders, as well as conceal my anxiety about the stranded seal.

"I think you'll be great," she says, and waves me off so she can focus on keeping the park visitors moving, rerouting the transportation for the special-access groups and generally making sure that the lost adolescent seal does not become a spectacle.

I meet my school group at the staging area, and I am relieved to see that there are three parent chaperones along with the teacher. I can't help but remember when Zach was these kids' age, bespectacled, inquisitive and chubby. I see a child like him in the group, a shy boy, a little shorter than the others. He has brought his own binoculars that he holds tightly to his chest.

I firm up my stance. I can feign authority if I need to. I ask the teacher for a head count, and try not to fiddle with my notes, or my cuffs or my zipper as the park interpreter tells the children to always stay behind me, to listen to what I have to say, not to chew gum, not to eat candy, not to remove anything from the trail. It helps having someone else go through the guidelines, and it sets me up as the leader.

We set off, keeping a steady pace until we reach the first turnout and the view of the lighthouse, the toppled tower and dilapidated keepers' dwellings out on the island. I explain how the lighthouse was built only after many shipwrecks at this point. There was a lighthouse at Pigeon Point, Pescadero, and one in Santa Cruz, but this stretch of the coast here at Año was unprotected. When the lighthouse was originally built here, it was with a fog light.

The kids ask who lives in the lightkeeper's house, and if we can go over. I break it to them that it is derelict, that only the scientists are allowed on the island to do research, and that although it looks exciting from here, it smells bad because of all the bird poo. I throw them another little tidbit about a stellar sea-lion skeleton in the bath. The creature must have climbed in and been unable to get out again.

I don't tell them about the lighthouse keepers who drowned trying to rescue the sailors of a ship in distress, and how the keepers' wives watched helplessly from the island. And I don't mention the seal that is stranded, though it is uppermost on my mind.

"Spanish explorer Sebastian Vizcaino sighted this land in 1603 while exploring the California coast. It was named Punta de Año Nuevo. Does anyone know what that translates as?" I ask them.

"New Year's Point," the studious little Zach-lookalike replies, bringing his binoculars down for a split second.

He is right, and I praise him for it.

As we descend the dunes, I spot a fully grown elephant seal in a puddle. I realize we are closer than the stipulated twenty-five feet away from him. It isn't ideal, but I don't want to disturb the rangers or the park interpreters, not in view of what they are dealing with.

"Hurry, hurry," I say to the children. But instead of my charges rushing, they slow down, they stop, they begin to snap pictures or even a few bursts of video to take away with them. It is as if the "monster" casts a hypnotic spell upon them. I should be stricter about it all, but I watch, I wait, and I gauge the elephant seal's body language. It is lying on its side and snoring; I trust we will all make it out of the park alive, and the little flutter of angst I feel, the slight tingle in my body, is nothing more than a low surge of excitement— job satisfaction.

I look around at this Jurassic Park, the wild landscape with the jagged mountains, the pterodactyl-like pelicans, and the lumbering elephant seals. I feel humbled that I am here, at this place that I might never have seen in another time, another age, another version of my life.

The children ask how deep the elephant seals dive, and I point to the mountain range behind us to demonstrate the comparison, telling them that the average dive is the same footage as the highest peak. I pass around a piece of elephant-seal fur, and the one seal whisker that I keep in a plastic bag in my jacket pocket. I tell them about Phyllis, an adult elephant-seal cow who was tracked swimming farther than any elephant seal had gone before, out into Japanese waters, and about TS (which stands for Toilet Seat), the poor elephant seal who was seen with a marine toilet seat that had been embedded into his neck. His name was later changed to TS Eliot because "Toilet Seat" was deemed too demeaning.

"After the seat was cut off and he was free to recover, he actually became an Alpha," I tell the children. "He came back year after year to the beach here. The docents knew it was TS because of the scars around his neck." I love this happy-ever-after story, how TS rose to the top despite such a difficult past.

The boys don't seem as inspired by the tale. They push and shove each other on the way back up over the dunes as the girls listen to music on their phones, sharing their headphones and giggling. Back at the staging area I wave them all off, watching the Zach-lookalike lag behind the group. He is a loner, a geek.

I check my phone out of habit, despite knowing there is no service here. I begin my search for Patrick. I want to know if the adolescent bull made it back to the beach. I don't see the seal anywhere.

"Do you know what happened to the stranded seal?" I ask the staff at the kiosk on my way out.

"We were told he was making his way back to the beach on the special-access road. He was sighted resting in the Brussels sprout field," they tell me. "That's all we know." It doesn't feel like enough to satisfy me. The elephant seal doesn't belong in the Brussels sprout field. It is an unfitting conclusion.

Once I reach Davenport and have cell service again, I get a call from Savanna.

"Zach has stopped taking his meds. He's either huddled under the blankets or staring into space," she tells me. "He doesn't want to wake up in the morning to do his college classes. He's hardly eating. He didn't want me to tell you."

I try to stay focused on the road, but I feel my stomach lurch. I was going to stop at the Swanton Berry Farm to get a scone and a cup of tea, but I drive right past it, Savanna's Texan accent loud in my earpiece.

"Will he talk to me?" I ask.

"No, and he won't talk to his doctor either," Savanna explains. "He's only getting out of bed to go to the bathroom, and he won't eat or drink unless I share my food with him. If I want something different or completely to myself, it causes an argument."

I feel like the storm I had been fearing—the one that had been gathering in the recesses of my mind, gaining pressure as it hovered over my hypothalamus, picking up wind speed between my ears—has finally broken. I imagine that the animals at the farm will sense it too, the opening of the heavens. They will retreat to the barns to take shelter. The sky will darken, and electricity will fork above the redwoods.

For Zach there will probably be a strange release, one I cannot ever fully understand. He has told Savanna that when he takes his prescribed drugs, he feels numb inside. He feels dead, and if he feels dead, he may as well be dead. The experience of psychosis is at least one with feelings, as extreme as they are. He knows he is alive in this state.

When the storm inside my body subsides, I am not as shocked as I am sad. Sad and disappointed. I am angry, too, but I don't know where to direct my rage. I hear the tiredness in Savanna's voice. Being young gives her more energy than I have. Being in love gives her hope and dreams. I know that this is all new to her. At some point the newness and novelty may wear thin, and she may leave.

I don't want her to go. I need her. She is giving me a breathing space of sorts, a chance to be a different kind of me. I ask if she has spoken to her parents, wondering about my responsibility, if I should try to tell them that their twenty-one-year-old daughter is having to deal with matters that are hard enough for me, thirty years her senior.

Savanna told me once how she always tried to fix other people's problems. She was the eldest child of four, all girls. The most sensible one. She was the good student at school, the designated driver when she and her friends went out to a party. She feels she can help Zach, force him to take his medication because he loves her. I see myself in her in so many ways, or I see her in myself. Both of us are large and nurturing, over-achievers.

I ask her to stay in touch, keep me posted, to keep herself safe. I also offer to fly down and support them both should it become necessary, although part of me feels it already is.

I say goodbye. I tell her I love her. I do. Of all the girlfriends that Zach has had, there is something about this girl that I want to protect. I think it is because I know her suffering, or I think I do. She is different from Zach's girlfriends in the past, or maybe it is that I am different in the way I perceive her. Her love appears more genuine, more generous, more authentic. It is a fierce, nurturing affection, like a mother's love. In years to come, I will listen to *On Being*, a podcast with Krista Tippett, who will interview an ex-hospice doctor about the subject of death and love. What I will learn is that romantic love has evolved out of the love a mother has for her baby. It is basically transference that we all practice, whether we are biological mothers or not. Some of us seem to just take to it more easily, more naturally, and Savanna strikes me as fitting that niche. I love Savanna because Zach loves her, and because I want to prove the world wrong, too. I want to show it with my angry fist raised high in the air, that Zach—like Ellyn Saks—can sustain a romantic attachment, and that he has so much to give to others in this world.

I feel myself try to conserve what is left of the day; the serene nature of the sun setting over the water, the kite-surfers flying in the wind, the moments of traveling on the road in what is surely one of the most gorgeous parts of the world. I am so very happy on the surface and so ultimately sad underneath. I am distraught on the one hand, yet joyful on the other; grateful for what I have, and mournful for what I have lost, all at the very same time.

11

ON THE STREETS

Savanna is interning at a music production company in downtown LA, but she returns in her lunch break to check on Zach and try to persuade him to eat, get up, take his pills. He agrees to take some, but not the full dose. It is a battle between them; a dance I know well because I have been the partner in it up until now.

I speak to Nance and decide not to rush down immediately, as I normally would, but rather to leave the two of them to try and manage, to see if Zach might be able to find a way to emerge from this. I promised him, and myself, this much.

After three days Savanna tells me that Zach is starting to refuse liquids too now, as well as food. I fly to Los Angeles and visit them at their studio in West Hollywood. Savanna has never seen Zach so removed from the world, never seen anyone this removed from the world.

My son has turned into a hibernating lizard, cold to the touch, and shocked into stillness. We wait one day, two days, and on the third we call the psychiatric evaluation team. They speak to Savanna who is brave as can be, but visibly upset. When they strap Zach into a wheelchair and put handcuffs on his wrists, she starts to cry. They load him into the ambulance and transfer him to a gurney. Savanna is allowed to accompany him. I wave goodbye and insist that they will be okay before I get into my car outside of their apartment. I allow myself to cry too, out of sight, under a beautiful palm on this gorgeous street in West Hollywood that I had prayed the storm wouldn't reach.

After Zach is admitted to the ward, Savanna comes back to our Hollywood home. She is too sad to be alone.

"The way they strapped him down in the ambulance, he couldn't even move his hands," she cries.

"I'm sorry," I say. I am so remorseful, so full of regret that it puts me off-kilter as I move around the house. I hold out my arms and hug Savanna as if she is my child too, equally wounded by the fallout. She sobs on my shoulder, and I wonder if I should have told her more that day on the beach, whether I could have prepared her.

"It's just that I've never been in an ambulance before," she reflects. "It was as if he were a criminal. He looked so scared. He had such fear in his eyes when the nurses tried to talk to him."

"Do you think you should talk to your family?" I ask, wondering if her mother might be able to offer her more support than I can. She shakes her head. Maybe she is nervous they will force her to return to Texas.

"I'm going to visit him twice a day, afternoon and evening sessions," she resolves, stemming her tears, "unless you want to go?"

"No, he'll prefer to see you," I admit.

"I'll take some time off work. I'll bake him his favorite cookies," she says. I can see she is exhausted by the trauma, which I know will stay with her now, in her body, and even though she is young and strong and moves around the world with ease, it will tally up a score within her psyche, and inform the way she makes sense of the world. She is like the medic in the war zone, rushing in while bombs are still falling, putting herself in the line of fire too. Once she is out of earshot, I put my head on the stainless-steel table in the basement kitchen and weep into a tea towel.

True to her word, Savanna keeps vigil at Zach's bedside at the hospital. He is diagnosed with dehydration and catatonia, and fed saline and anti-anxiety drugs through a drip. Savanna's presence, along with the pecan tassies (an old southern recipe), cream puffs and chicken pot pies that she bakes for him so lovingly, seem to bring him around.

On one occasion she comes back more upset than ever. "I just lay down next to him on the bed, that's all," she whimpers. "The nurse on duty saw us on the surveillance camera. She told me off. She said it was against the rules, and I couldn't visit if I did that again."

Poor Savanna. Poor Zach. Just when human contact is needed, it is forbidden. For a time I hold my breath, cross my fingers, try to be close enough to support them both, but distant enough to let them have some autonomy, a rarity on the psych ward.

Zach is released with a poor prognosis. Savanna tries, they both do, but Zach hates the side effects of the drugs more than ever. He goes out less and less into the world, which isn't easy for Savanna, who is new to Los Angeles and everything it has to offer, especially the music scene. I see their partnership start to fray around the edges, both dejected and tested by the ravages of a love story gone wrong. Savanna's internship ends, and without work and money for rent in Los Angeles, her family beckons her home.

Zach goes to the park that he and Savanna used to go to together on the days when he felt well enough to be outside, only now he goes there alone. The entrance is close to the apartment they once shared, but had to give up, and she isn't there anymore. I try to imagine what it must feel like to be Zach right now, fresh out of the psychiatric ward, on-again-off-again with the powerful drugs; labeled with an illness, a disorder; on a government benefit; with a girlfriend who has left him and become yet another ex; one more thing that once was, past tense, no more.

It is dark when I find him lying on top of a picnic table.

"I'm still here, Zach," I say, and perhaps that makes it worse, because who, as a young adult, wants their mother as their only person, as their salvation. In psychiatry it is the family that is often blamed, thought to bring about relapse—especially the mother, always the mother. The nurses and doctors are taught this model during their training. They have charts to fill, boxes to tick that document us as too hostile, too emotional, too over-involved. It strikes me as contradictory that the biomedical model insists that the illness is nobody's fault, rather a chemical imbalance, a brain disorder, and yet the family is still deemed to be instrumental in causing relapse. How can I be blameless on the one hand, and culpable on the other?

Back at our Hollywood house, Zach returns to the old green couch. The upholstery sags, and there are stains on the arms.

He raises his head off the pillow. "I don't want to live like this. I want to die. Can you take me to Oregon and help me?" he begs. "Surely I have the right to request that, don't I?"

"Oh, Z," is all I can manage.

"Euthanasia is legal there," he insists.

I am crushed by the enormity of his distress. It seems surreal to hear these words come out of the mouth of someone so young, my precious son who wanted to live more than anyone I had ever met just six years ago.

It feels like too much has happened for me to make it better by scratching his scalp like I did when he was a baby, or by buying him a Subway sandwich when he was a pre-teen and bargaining with him to stay here. I don't even know if listening is enough, because of how wrenching it is for me to hear these words. I just sit with him and put my hand on his arm, as if he really is already dying. He doesn't eat much. The drugs clearly aren't helping.

"I don't want to see any more doctors. I've had enough of hospitals," he says. His voice sounds so weak. He closes his eyes, and a tiny teardrop escapes him.

I leave him alone and go to my room. It is a risk, not doing anything, but I feel that forcing him back into the hospital is an even greater one. A pressure wells up in my chest. I need to release it. I call my NAMI mums.

"It's good he can tell you these things," one of them reassures me on the phone.

"That is so great that he can cry," my friend Janey says. I have known her since before Zach was born, and the fact that she is based in London means I can call her in the early hours of the morning here, when the rest of California is fast asleep.

Nance is stretched so thin with work and caring for her mum, yet she helps me find a board and care home for Zach. It is close to us in Northern California. She goes to look at it in her lunch break and speaks to the managers.

"You know, it doesn't smell bad, and they have gardens and a little black cat," she tells me. "They feed the residents healthy food, and they don't leave them to sleep all day."

"Did you check for bedbugs?" I ask. We know that this is a common problem in this kind of accommodation. "What about street drugs?"

"Well, they aren't going to advertise those problems, are they? Tan, it's not going to be perfect."

I know that a board and care facility is not going to be perfect. It is often a warehouse for those that the world doesn't know what to do with anymore. I never thought we would get to this place.

The staff at this home say that they support their residents to go to the gym, to college, to work. I wonder, though, I truly do. Words are cheap. Nance sends us the website for the accommodation, and I ask Zach to sit up and look at the pictures.

"You'll be so close to us all up there," I say, in the hope he will be encouraged.

It seems Zach has other ideas. Three weeks after Savanna has left, he doesn't come home. I call the only two acquaintances he has left in the area. They haven't seen him. I check his phone, his Facebook, his bank account. Nothing. I am frantic. I drive to the park and check every path and picnic table. I visit the encampments on Cahunega and Hollywood Boulevard. I try to convince myself that he has made a friend, and is warm and safe inside his or her tent.

After four nights of Zach having been missing, I am so fraught, I call Nance and say, "I want to drive to Skid Row just in case he's found his way there."

"No, don't," she says. We both know that Skid Row, in downtown Los Angeles, is one of the most drug-ridden and violent places, especially once the sun goes down and the homeless shelters lock their doors for the night. But it is also a community where some of the most incredible healing takes place because of the concentration of services in the area. It is both things, but still Nance is nervous about me going there.

"I can stay in my car," I tell her. "I'll drive slowly so I can see out of the window."

"If you have to go, wait until daylight, and take someone with you hon. Please."

Nance's sentiment makes sense, even though the long, dark nights are the hardest, the times that I want to be out looking for him the most. Besides anything else, driving and looking for a missing person simultaneously is difficult. I follow Nance's advice and wait the night out, restless and tense. The next morning I enlist the help of Carolyn, the acupuncturist. She doesn't bring sage this time, but she closes her eyes and asks our angels, the ones we'd prayed to before, to guide us to Zach. I want to ask her why the angels would let him take off like this in the first place, but I focus on driving, or I try to, though I know my steering is a little shaky.

The angels don't deliver, so that night I go to the police station with a recent picture of Zach. He has shaved his head and grown his beard. When I tell the officer Zach's age, he looks impatient, weary. He looks like he isn't taking it seriously, despite me saying that my son is a vulnerable adult.

"Just so you are aware, Ma'am," he says in a Southern accent, "if we find him and he is neither homicidal nor suicidal, we are not obligated to inform you of his whereabouts, not unless he gives us permission."

Thirty thousand people are living on the streets of LA, and I dare not look up how many of them die out there each year. I don't sleep. I call the psychiatric hospitals. I call the police to see if he has been arrested. I can't bring myself to call the morgues, although I know other parents in my situation who have done so. I rely increasingly on them now—their calm voices, the knowledge that they have walked in my shoes.

Dale flies down and takes over the driving. We search more parks, more sidewalks, and Santa Monica Beach. I want to believe that Zach will survive this, that he will find a way to contact us, but I conceive of darker possibilities, where my family comes out from England for Zach's funeral. My brother is on one side of me, my sister on the other, holding me up. Nance and Dale are behind me in case I should topple backward. My dark glasses hide my eyes and the shame in them. Under the shades my gaze is glassy, vacant. I don't know how to focus on the world without my son.

Two weeks later, he is spotted on a neighbor's surveillance camera: thin, filthy, without a jacket or possessions. He walks slowly and pisses on the driveway, but he is alive.

I place a sleeping bag, clothes and provisions outside on our hillside deck. If he comes back and is too scared to come in, at least he will find what he needs to stay fed, hydrated, and warm at night when the temperature drops dramatically.

At 2 a.m. the security light goes on. There he is. I hardly recognize him. He looks startled and dirty, his eyes sunken, his face like a puffer fish. At first he tries to run away, but I call his name. "Zigs, it's me, Mum."

I throw away his filthy clothes and his shoes, the soles worn down to almost nothing. I lead him to the shower and make him scrub until the water runs clear. I feed him, put him to bed and ice his swollen feet.

He is home, but I feel changed. I have looked his mortality in the face and survived it.

I know we cannot stay here in this city of angels who do not answer our prayers, this place that has almost destroyed us.

The next morning, I stuff the car with Zach's belongings and head toward the Bay Area. As we merge from the 170 to the 5 North, Zach describes the nights he spent on the streets. "I felt trapped in a time warp," he says. "I thought the cars on Sunset Boulevard were operating on autopilot and would brake if I got in their way. I had to keep running to escape from one city zone to another, to stay in this century."

It is a lot for me to consider, especially while navigating five lanes of traffic and the freeway signs, but it explains why he lost all his belongings, why his feet were so swollen and the soles of his shoes had worn thin enough to see daylight through them.

"Why didn't you come home sooner?" I ask, revisiting the panic I had lived with. He tries to fashion an answer, but he is distracted by me stretching my fingers out on the wheel. It unnerves him. He thinks I am signaling to other drivers.

I still my hands and keep them at ten and two on the wheel.

"I wanted to come home, but I thought you had sold the house and didn't live there anymore. I even asked a policeman to call you for me, but he refused. He just gave me the address of a local shelter for the homeless."

I feel my brow furrow; now it is my turn to be confused. I bite my lip and stare ahead as we climb the Grapevine, the dramatic mountain pass that separates the Tehachapis from the San Emigdios. As we descend into Tejon Ranch, Zach drops his head and confesses how he felt like a human experiment that had reached hell on earth.

"There were some good people that bought me food and water," he says softly.

It is this that hits me hardest. I want to thank these people, know them, pay them in kind for the water that kept my son hydrated in the dust bowl of Los Angeles.

I sigh heavily and feel the seatbelt contain me. I'm so thankful he found a way to reach the light, to find his way back. I will never know if it was motherly love, my prayers, the kind souls on the streets who fed and watered him, or his will to survive that returned him to me. As we speed through the San Joaquin Valley, past endless fields of spinach and artichokes, the how and the why don't seem to matter the way they used to. I know I need to embrace change, to give up my constant questioning and just say thank you.

HOME

"Please, take me back to England," Zach says. "Or just put me on the plane and I can stay with dad."

He is lying on our couch at the cabin, shoes and jacket on as usual, as if he may need to make a quick getaway, despite not having a car and being two miles up a mountain road, sixteen hundred feet above sea level.

We go through the reasons that he can't stay with his dad. His dad has chronic obstructive pulmonary disease and lives in senior living accommodation. He asks again and again, as if enough pleading will change my answer. He badgers his dad, too, on video chats. He is desperate. England, his safe place for much of his childhood, is something to hold on to.

We have tried different things since coming north after Zach's two weeks on the streets. A little studio in Seaside, close to Dale. A shack in Santa Cruz near the beach. The board and care home Nance found that denied it had bedbugs, even when Zach was smothered in red welts from the bites. A private residential treatment program that helped with structure but harmed with copious amounts of prescribed drugs.

In between these futile attempts, and a few more short-lived but wretched hospitalizations, Zach stays with us here at the cabin, mostly because I can't bear the thought of him becoming homeless again. He talks about the people on the streets, and some nights he goes to visit them. "They are my people. They are free," he tells me.

It is during this time that we find a psychologist called Daisy.

For some years now, Zach has been reluctant to talk to psychologists, psychiatrists, therapists, doctors, social workers, care coordinators or anyone else about anything to do with his prescribed drugs, his mind, his mood, his diagnosis. Tired of the form-filling, the pill-pushing, the questions about his voices and visions and extreme states, he has resorted to staying away from professionals and the language that so many of them use to describe him. So I am surprised when he agrees to meet and talk to Daisy.

Daisy strikes me as different from the moment I see her website. Her words are thoughtful, and I hear a lightness in her voice. I think it must be this that draws Zach through her office door the first time, and that brings him back. She wears a t-shirt with capped sleeves. Her biceps are strong. Zach trusts her quickly. We both do. Like him, she received a diagnosis of schizoaffective disorder as a teen. Over the months that Zach and I work with her, we learn how she was fed a cocktail of antipsychotic drugs that left her unable to function. When her psychiatrist refused to help, she began the secretive, painstaking process of weaning herself off her drugs: weighing, measuring and shaving them down until she was able to find her way back to a sense of self that was worth living for. She understands Zach's sense of feeling so numb that life has no point to it, because she has experienced the same emptiness, a kind of chemical lobotomy.

Zach had always wanted to quit his psychotropic drugs, but we had never met anyone who believed it was possible. After so many years of him taking so many different drugs, we learn that other people, some of whom call themselves survivors, manage to stop or decrease their prescribed drugs and regain some autonomy.

Zach meets some of them at a workshop in Oakland, although he decides to leave it early. "It's just a bit overwhelming," he tells me when he calls.

The overwhelm is real for me, too, but also uplifting, enlightening, hopeful. We learn about something called Open Dialogue, a model of therapy developed in Finland, a country once renowned for its high suicide rates. Based on family communication groups along with minimal or no use of psychiatric drugs, it has been credited with successfully treating psychosis. It is about listening and guiding, rather than forcing.

Zach was never able to receive psychological therapy while he was detained in the psych wards, because professionals often maintained that someone who is acutely psychotic should not begin this form of treatment. Conversely Open Dialogue practitioners meet the person and those close to them wherever they are in their journey, looking at what underlies the psychosis, making meaning of the voices. The concept makes so much sense. I remember what it meant to be heard at the age of nineteen. I had gone with friends to a Campaign for Nuclear Disarmament rally at RAF Molesworth in Cambridgeshire, where American nuclear weapons were stationed. We got soaked and muddy as we wandered, coatless, around the perimeter, chanting and full of rage. Soon it was dark, and we were freezing. The Quakers from the local parish found us, fed us, clothed us and warmed us up with hot cocoa while listening deeply to our innermost fears about nuclear war and the end of the world. I have liked the Quaker Church ever since. Natural open dialogue practitioners.

•

California has traditionally been seen as a place of new ideas, from the phenomenological writings of the mid-twentieth century to the present-day entrepreneurial spirit, so I am surprised it has taken us this long to discover someone like Daisy. She tells us about Norway, where mental health laws permit psychiatric hospitalization with optional drug treatment. Zach also finds out about Hearing Voices, a peer-led group that supports and aids those who live with this experience. Daisy says it was the first place she felt heard and understood, and where her experience made sense. Voice hearing isn't always distressing. It is much more common than we realize, and many people live comfortably with their voices. Some even feel that their voices are a spiritual entity, a gift.

As the dry, hot summer of 2019 announces itself, I calculate that a decade has slipped by since that night in the laundry room in Hollywood. I will often regret not meeting Daisy earlier, but I know that regret is the soul's worst enemy. After less than a year of working together, Daisy announces that she needs to leave California to handle a family emergency. I would follow her if I could, but I also realize she has set me on a new path, one more aligned with Zach. We now have real, living examples of what it means to crack but not break, to break through but not down, to understand what it is to emerge spiritually from chaos with a richer understanding of what it means to be human.

As for Zach, he has permission for the first time to be his authentic self without fear of being sent to the hospital. His connection with Daisy means he can look at what happened to him rather than what is wrong with him. It is such a freeing narrative. Nobody can take that away from either of us. The fact remains, however, that Zach has experienced a decade of coercive treatment; he still wants to numb his pain. Healing might be a lifetime's journey for Zach, for me, for our family. What we are trying to do is enormous, to make the past inter-generational trauma of our ancestors stop with us.

At the cabin, I move outside to sit on the deck. The rooster crows. The goats clamber down the hillside into the meadow.

"Come sit with me," I call to Zach through the screen door.

He joins me, along with Midge, the scruffy little mutt that we recently adopted from the Monterrey animal shelter. She is gray and feisty, like Belle only smaller. Oaks and Douglas firs shelter us from the sun as we perch on the redwood slats. Our feet rest on the step below, just out of reach of the emu, who likes to peck at us if given the opportunity. Normally I laugh at him as he sashays past, feathers splayed, looking for a mate. But today I am struggling, the events of yesterday still sinking in.

I had found Nance weeping in her locked car, the only private space she could find. Her pale complexion was blotched red, and black mascara smudged her knuckles and cheeks. She wasn't coping, she said, not with her mother dying, not with Zach being at the cabin. It would be easier for her to be alone.

I have seen her cry fewer times than the number of years we have been together, so this hit hard—the pain of not being needed or wanted, especially during a time of great upheaval. Nance had been my wife and co-parent for the last seventeen years, yet somehow, as I had moved closer to Zach, she had backed further away until she could let go enough to love him at a distance. Her words numbed me.

I watch Zach's cat Richard Parker weave around his master's legs. Zach strokes the creature's scruffy face. He is most at home in nature with animals, more at peace in his body—like most of us, I suppose. Nance and I have spent many days wishing that this little parcel of land at Lakeview Bird Farm belonged to us, so we could build a cabin or a trailer here for Zach; his own space. But we don't own the land, and even if we did build him a home here, Zach still has fears and voices and extreme states that leave us all exhausted. Daisy has helped me find agricultural communities run with a compassionate focus, places where organic food is served and drugs are tapered under supervision, where staff and clients live and work together as family. But the price tag—oh my god, the price tag. Thousands and thousands of dollars.

As dusk starts to settle over the farm, creating shadows behind the horse trailer and the barn, I wonder if this is the push I need, to take Zach home to England. I bite the inside of my cheek as I consider living with an ocean and a continent between Nance and me. I think about Gordon, who has separated from his wife, the mother of his two youngest children. Can he become the kind of father to Zach that he couldn't be in the past? Zach has spent time with Gordon in the UK since his first experience of psychosis, but he never stayed for longer than a few months at a time. There was his United States immigration status to consider, but mostly he wanted to get back to us—his solid, safe family—in America. Now there are more periods of uncertainty. "Where would be the best place for me, Mum," he has asked so many times, "a country where I won't be hunted down and taken away?"

I want it to be England. I dream it could be England. I pray that Zach won't be second fiddle in his father's life and that they can forge a closeness that will make Zach feel unconditionally loved. I contact Gordon, who agrees that Zach can stay with him for two weeks at the most, as this is the maximum time that he is allowed to host guests for. I will look for a little place close by. See how things go. I book our flight before I can change my mind.

The mountain cabin in Los Gatos, our once so cherished symbol of refuge, feels smaller than ever before we leave. Noise travels easily in a

450-square-foot open-plan structure. We hear Zach shout in his sleep, and we wake each time he rises to eat, drink, shower in the early hours when he is most restless. I remember now how the Craigslist ad had stated that this accommodation was only suitable for one person. Now that one person will be Nance.

During our last night together, I try to make peace. "I will definitely come back and help you take care of your mum, once I've set everything up for Zach," I whisper in the darkness, "let his darn father take a turn." It feels insincere even as it comes out of my mouth. How will I leave Zach? How does a mother ever leave her child, even if he is a grown man?

Dale drives us to the airport and helps us check in. "See you, cat," he says, punching Zach's bicep. "Give my love to everyone." I hug Dale and watch him walk away, his fair, sun-bleached hair sticking out from his beanie. It is just us. Me and Zach.

Zach is nervous about flying, about the number of people in the departure lounge, the chatter and announcements and harsh fluorescent lights. I focus on keeping us both calm, remembering the times he has been too scared to cross the gangway between the terminal and the plane. When we board, I hold my breath. Zach squeezes the armrest as we taxi down the runway, his eyes wide with apprehension. I am churned up too, turbulent like the weather above us.

Regret, gratitude and guilt all rise in me. Regret that Nance and I cannot be together through our shared hardship. Gratitude that she has been honest about her limits, so I can be truthful about mine. Guilt that she must take care of her dying mother alone.

The steward asks if I would like anything to drink with my meal. I choose Pinot Noir, even though I hate the taste of it, hate the taste of almost all alcohol. It sloshes around on my tray table with every bump in the sky. When I finally down it I feel warm, and the worries start to peel away. I put my head against the window. Zach has managed to fall asleep. He looks young, peaceful, boyish. A shave always takes years off him. Seeing him like this reminds me of the flight we made seventeen years ago from London to Los Angeles, from our old home to our new one, the opposite of this journey. Zach, at twelve, staring quietly out of the little porthole window at the sea and so much uninhabited land, enjoying the airplane food with abandon. Dale at thirteen, barely eating, switching channels on his individual seat-back entertainment screen.

Me, anticipating a better life for my boys.

As we get closer to our destination, I wonder what we will face in the Old Country. We are citizens, but no longer residents. We have relatives, but we have been mostly away from them for almost two decades.

The sun sets somewhere below us—I think it might be Iceland. As I fall into a weird, alcohol-induced half sleep at altitude, I think about the elephant seals and their long biannual migrations. Every year, for as long as they live, they are driven by evolution, by some instinctive rhythm that they feel in their body. It brings them thousands of miles, back through the water, to the exact same breeding ground where they were born, the beach that, for two or three months each year, is their home.

13

THE SWAFF

Summer 2019

We land. We are exhausted and jetlagged. The car rental company wants to charge us three hundred pounds for insurance because my current driver's license is from the USA and not the UK. I cancel the reservation, but Zach is scared to get on the train. He says this isn't the same England. He is right, in a way. We are home, but we are strangers in a foreign world. The money looks unfamiliar. The roundabouts are dizzying. The notion of starting all over again, of trying to establish what Zach needs, what we both need, makes my head hurt.

We manage to find the right train, but Zach sits far away from me in a different part of the carriage. He looks pale and tired. I keep my eye on him in case he gets off the train and wanders away. He might lie down on the platform, unwilling to move. These are all things he has done before, when his voices and fears become unbearable.

As we head north-east, the countryside becomes a tapestry of flat, green squares and rectangles. Parcels of land that have been divided for eons, all the way back to feudal times. It seems odd without the Santa Cruz mountains. It feels like we could tip off this saucer of land. There is nothing to hold us in.

Fire season will begin soon in the dry, barren parts of California, where no rain has fallen for months. Here it is greener, but sticky with humidity and a temperature that is, absurdly enough, higher than in California. The UK is not used to dealing with extreme weather and has no air-conditioning or other measures in place to combat it.

We take the bus to Swaffham. It trundles along the country lanes, through villages with cobbled stones and thatched cottages. Swaffham, where Zach's father, aunt and half-siblings reside, is an old market town that was famous for its sheep and wool industry. Large houses served as destinations for Londoners who came here for soirees. It was the childhood home of Howard Carter, the man who led the excavation of Tutankhamun's tomb.

At first it is hard to imagine such a glorious past for this town. All I see are the multitudes of charity shops, greasy spoon cafés and karaoke pubs. Perhaps a part of me is angry and I have just repressed it until now. Could it be rage manifesting as my prejudice against Swaffham, rather than angst toward Gordon, who has been able to hide away and live a life that is less concerned with Zach? I know this is true, because before long I will come to cherish the Swaff, as the locals refer to it. I will find the back cobbled alleys with listed cottages in the conservation area, acres of pristine woodland, and people with whom I will forge deep friendships.

Gordon opens the door and bellows, "Son of mine." I stand back in the small, cluttered living room and watch them hug. "Oh, look at you, young fella-me-lad," Gordon says, taking in how much Zach has grown in the three or four years since they have last seen each other. Father and son. Maybe it's the jet lag, the heat and the time that has passed, but something in me gives a bit, like an old chair with worn webbing.

"Aye, bloody hell, come in. I made you a sausage sandwich," Gordon tells Zach. "Want one?" he asks me. I turn my nose up.

"No, you're alright." I say, imitating his accent.

The one-bedroom flat is smoky and smells of grease and tobacco. I sink into an enormous orange chair in the corner of the living room and accept a cup of tea, weak and milky, in a tannin-stained mug. It pulls me back to 1984, when Gordon and I first met. I used to stay at his studio apartment—even though I wasn't meant to. I would climb in through the back window after dark, share a brew of Bolton broken orange pekoe, a bacon sandwich and a few cigs—Silk Cut. I slept with him in his single bed under the Karl Marx poster, next to the vertical record player, leaving early the next morning before the staff arrived at the building.

Everything has changed but the smells are similar, and there are still rules.

"Two weeks, Zach. That's your lot, or I'll get into trouble," Gordon reminds him. The regulations of the senior living complex make my ex seem old before his time. Old and different. This man, who once prided himself on being a northerner, a socialist, a bloke who said southerners were soft bloody Tories, now talks about how he voted for Brexit. Change. So much change. The only constant in life.

After his two weeks are up, Zach joins me in a twin room at a Georgian hotel in town. There are no Open Dialogue or Hearing Voices groups here. On Sunday we go to a Norman church, enormous and impressive with a vaulted ceiling and stained-glass windows. It is in the center of the town, surrounded by headstones that have been dug up and rearranged in straight lines so the grass can be mown between them. It seems like sacrilege to have disturbed the hallow ground. The church service is mostly a lecture, and a couple of hymns, a far cry from the listening, silent Quakers.

I find some progressive clinicians in London who are doing private work in the field of avatar therapy and the like. Zach doesn't want to see anyone. "Not yet," he tells me. "Not just yet."

Soon he begins to withdraw, to visit Gordon less, to stay in bed. The voices in his head grow louder and more demeaning. Help is harder to find than I envisaged. We are eventually given an appointment with the local mental health team. We are assigned a social worker who is brusque, and says that Zach might not be entitled to NHS provision because we haven't been in the country very long. This is despite me offering to pay.

We find an agency that is funded by Mind, one of the largest mental health charities in the UK. They allocate us an advocate called Elaine, for an hour a week. I like Elaine. She is soft-spoken and attentive. She asks Zach if he wants to attend any social groups or take part in the local gardening project. He tries, but he is tired. We both are. Weary with an uppercase W.

My sister is right. Things have changed in England since we left seventeen years ago. There are long waiting lists for treatments, and renting private accommodation proves difficult, especially because Zach has no job, and no history of a job or a prior tenancy in the UK. Gordon has lived in Swaffham for twenty years. This qualifies Zach to be able to sign up with the local GP and apply for benefits, but the question of housing is more elusive. We move into a Victorian Airbnb cottage which is affordable because it is off-season.

On the other side of the Atlantic, Barb is dying, but I do not return. She passes with Nance by her side, and still I don't go back. I listen to Nance cry on the phone in the moments after her mum has gone. I recognize the release as well as the pain. Nance agrees it is more important that I remain here with Zach rather than attend the funeral in person, so on the day of the service she connects with me by video, screwing her phone to a tripod at the back of the church hall. I feel guilty; I feel so far away. It is late for me in the UK because of the time difference, and I cannot hear very well. I speak to family after the service and apologize for not being there.

I might not understand it in that moment, but Zach and I are enmeshed, entangled, and it is no wonder. We have come all this way together. I can't let him go. To whom? Where? There is no safety net here, or in America. It is mostly us against the world, or that's what it feels like. I know that Nance has us in her heart and that she and I are still in it to win it, as Dale once said about our relationship, but she is wounded now too, and so far away that it stings like the nettles in Epping Forest.

It is shortly after Barb's death, when I ask Gordon to have Zach, and I make a quick bolt out to California to see Nance and collect Midge. Nance looks thinner and older, a frailty born of watching her mother suffer. The week is one of worry. Zach is struggling without me. Midge needs a health certificate and all kinds of documents in order to fly back to the UK. It is a blur of jet lag and dizzying sadness before I am back in Norfolk again with a puppy to add to the mix.

As winter approaches, Zach wants help. In my mind it is simple. We need community, Sangha, as it is known in the Buddhist tradition. People who can surround us, even in our hardest moments, and be with us. But here in Norfolk, without a car, and with Zach still finding it hard to completely trust anyone other than me, community is a slippery concept to bring to fruition. Most folks are too busy or stretched to find time for themselves, let alone others. Inevitably, what is offered to Zach is the same as it has always been—drugs, and a nurse to inject them into his arm. He agrees, desperate for relief.

Within three months, the antipsychotic is raised to the maximum dose. Soon, the side effects become worse than the psychotic experiences themselves. At this point, Zach asks to admit himself voluntarily to the new psychiatric ward in King's Lynn. It takes many weeks of trying. The crisis team come out every night and crowd into the tiny, quaint living room of the cottage. They say that there isn't a single hospital bed available in the county. One night I think I hear them say there isn't a single bed in the whole country, but perhaps I misunderstood.

Life feels surreal. Mostly because of broken nights of sleep, but also because I cannot believe that someone suffering such distress has to wait so interminably long.

It is just after Christmas when Zach is finally admitted to the ward. We are pleasantly surprised. The place is so recently built it still smells of paint and newness. But I am perplexed that a new unit has been constructed at what must have been a cost of millions of pounds, yet there are still not enough beds.

The furniture is soft, and it isn't weighted or screwed to the floor. The patients have the means to make tea and coffee and help themselves to snacks. There are no long, dank corridors that patients wander up and down. There is no screaming or banging on the walls. Instead of hospital gowns or pajamas, patients wear their own clothes. The plan is that Zach will start a trial of clozapine, a drug that is used more routinely here. The staff believe it might help him in a way the other drugs haven't.

For a time, I consider how I had held out real hope for alternative treatments for Zach. It feels like I am selling out, and reminds me of when I was pregnant with Dale. I had wanted a home birth with a radical midwife. My plea went unheard by the NHS, so I compromised by taking prenatal classes with the National Childbirth Trust and writing a birth plan. I wanted dim lights, a beanbag, soft music and the option to kneel or squat to give birth. But when I got to Homerton Hospital that all went out the window: I shouted too loudly, feared too much, hurt too badly. I was strapped to a monitor, feet in stirrups, numbed from the waist down and kept quiet with drugs. This birth was out of my hands, out of the hands of my midwives. It was the preserve of the male obstetricians. Dale was ripped out of me by a process known as ventouse, a vacuum extraction, then whisked away to the special care baby unit. I wanted to run after him, but my legs didn't work. I was so torn that I couldn't sit down comfortably afterward for months.

A natural childbirth, at home, with radical midwives, using a birthing pool or a birthing stool, with the ability to sway or dance or be scared and comforted, was out of vogue back in the late eighties. It was seen as alternative—dangerous, even—especially for the working class.

We have lost the ability to be with each other in our moments of greatest pain and life-and-death experiences. Opting for drugs and the relative "safety" of a hospital is seen as a natural response to trauma or existential crisis or spiritual emergency. There is nothing less natural, though, than psychotropic drugs and an artificial, locked environment. Friends and family tell me that at least Zach is safe in the hospital, that it is the best place for him, that the staff there know what they are doing. I nod. I think it is odd that they don't see any evidence of dissonance in my eyes.

I give up the Victorian Airbnb, which I can't afford forever, and move around the home counties staying with family and friends, and commuting to see Zach. But the day the drug regime is meant to start, Zach changes his mind. He looks up the drug online and reads that clozapine can cause urinary incontinence, drooling, tachycardia. It has the worst withdrawal effects if stopped and is associated with extreme weight gain, enough to cause diabetes.

I understand his concern. It is predictable at this point. I feel like we are cornered in a damned-if-we-do, damned-if-we-don't scenario. I have to accept that mental health care in this little leafy corner of

England is not quite as progressive as I had hoped, or as its reputation in America suggested. It looks prettier and more colorful on the ward, but the archaic paradigm is as unchanged as ever.

Zach halts the trial, and asks to stay longer in the hospital without taking medication. The staff tell him he is in a psychiatric ward, not a hotel, and that unless he complies with drug treatment, he cannot stay any longer. He is discharged into a bed-and-breakfast accommodation for the homeless in Dereham, half an hour by bus from his father's home. I think about the hospitals Daisy told us about in Norway that don't force drugs, or Trieste, where there is no psychiatric incarceration at all. The UK has a somewhat less criminalizing approach to mental health than America, but there are still very rigid ways of treating people that are not necessarily in their best interests. Mostly, I think about the therapeutic farm communities we can't afford and the thought that maybe one day we could start our own.

Zach's new accommodation is part of what was once an old stable block that was built in 1757. The front of the room butts up against an austere concrete parking lot. Zach's lodging and the other five dwellings in the low-slung building belong to the King's Head hotel, an inn with a bar and kitchen that serves roast dinners on Sundays.

The only window in the 150-square-foot space looks out onto the hotel gardens where picnic benches, tables and a swing set for the patrons' kids are arranged. It has no kitchen, no washing machine, no bathtub and no internet. Under his sink, a strip of Formica has been ripped clean away, exposing bare chipboard. The narrow single bed has a sagging mattress and a quilt that appears to be disintegrating.

"We don't really fix up the rooms too much because they just get damaged, and then the council has to pay," the manager says when she sees me eyeing a hole the size of a fist in the back of the bathroom door.

As small and unkempt as it is, it is a roof over his head.

"The fact that it's temporary means that if you keep it clean, and do well, you will get rehomed," I tell Zach. I don't tell him that I have spoken to the couple in the room next door, and despite one of them having severe mobility as well as developmental challenges, they have been waiting for permanent accommodation for eighteen months.

I bed down with friends and family as I wait for Nance to arrive. She is coming here for work. I want to return to California with her, to see Dale and my elephant seals. I know the separation will be challenging but I feel burned out. I yearn for respite, for somebody else to take over from me and take care of Zach, even if it is just for a short time.

My last stop before meeting up with Nance is with Janey, my friend of thirty-one years, and her wife Jo. On my first morning in their airy Victorian home in London, I put the kettle on before taking Midge out into the narrow garden that backs onto the railway line. The 7:14 trundles past on the way from Chingford to Liverpool Street. Midge runs to me for protection.

"It's okay, silly goose," I tell her. "It's just a train."

I scoop her up into my arms. Together we go back inside, and I pour the tea. Drinking tea, lots of it, comes naturally to me now. It reminds me of my past, and of mum, who made tea for every occasion. I am just three miles from where she lived in one direction and the same distance from where she died in the other. It is a bright February morning, almost sixteen years to the day since she passed. It feels like yesterday. It feels like a lifetime ago. Zach wants to visit Chingford Hall Estate, the spot where our tower block once stood before it was razed to the ground.

I am putting the milk back in the fridge when he Skypes me. The call is on speaker.

"Zigster."

"Where are you?" he asks.

"I'm still in London."

"Can I come and stay there?"

"Not right now."

"Do you think it's the same Chingford," he asks, in all seriousness, "or does it feel fake?"

"It's definitely the same Chingford," I assure him. "It has changed though, over the years, like everything. You will see."

"I don't believe it. As soon as the warm weather comes, I want to go homeless, to find my people."

Zach switches on his camera and invites me to do the same. I see his face, his hair buzzed short with clippers he bought from Boots. His glasses have been taped together with a band-aid. He had an appointment for an eye test at Specsavers on the high street, but the optometrist wanted to know where he lived and who his GP was, so he never went back. I see discarded food wrappers and containers and uneaten food in the frame behind him.

The camera blurs and freezes.

"I love you Zigs. I'll call you back," I say, hoping he can still hear me.

I remember the times when I would stay on the phone for ages trying to encourage him to call a helpline, see his therapist, take his psychiatric drugs, buy supplements, cut out sugar or gluten, eat more fish, red meat, pistachios, pray, get some sleep, wake up earlier in the day, surf, walk, jog, go to a meeting with NAMI, AA, join a chess group, read, write, admit himself to the hospital, connect with friends, family. The advice was endless. We are both tired of me repeating it ad nauseam. The more I push something, the more Zach resists. The laws of inertia are strong this way.

Zach calls back almost immediately.

"What was the name of the first dog we got from Battersea?"

"Max."

"What did we used to do on Friday nights before we moved to America?"

"Have takeaway supper and rent a movie from Blockbuster."

"When did Belle die?"

"Seventeen months ago."

He clicks the camera off without saying goodbye. He is reality testing, asking me questions that he believes only I will know, something that one of his therapists taught him to do during the early months of his experience of psychosis. This way, he hopes to prove I am his real mother, not a robot, and he is himself, not an alien. My answers do not always satisfy him, but I hope they will today, at least for now.

I take my friends up their tea and thank them again for allowing me to share their refuge. I perch on the Ercol couch in the bedroom—a gorgeous piece of furniture found in the street and refurbished by them—and watch as Midge greets their black labradoodle. The two beasts nip each other and wrestle. We laugh at their small, innocent pleasure.

"I'm going to take these two blighters out," I say, pointing at the animals.

I want to be strong in every sense of the word when Nance arrives, to show her I am coping. That I am a healthy equal. That I am assertive enough to leave Zach and return with her to America, to our life together as a couple. I have read that when one person has to care for another in their relationship, as I felt Nance did with me emotionally, it causes the kind of imbalance that creates dysfunction. Being with my wife is what I hope for. It is what I have always hoped for. But I am also painfully aware of my reality, and the fact that Zach may need me, until his life is less unsettled. Again, I find myself trying to find a way to be with two different people separated by an ocean, a feat as daunting as it was six months ago, six years ago, a phenomenon I cannot pull off unless I can compress time or space or both. An impossible feat.

For now, I am walking every day, hoping my physical vigor will translate into a resilient psyche. I pull on the boots that I bought last winter. Jo puts a handful of dog treats in my pocket before I brace the outside world.

THE LANGHAM

M y phone pings, and I see a message from Gordon. He has a chest infection and cannot help with Zach. I picture him on the living room floor with his felt-tip pens and sketchpad, working on his abstract tree series. I see the pouch of tobacco, filters and rolling papers by his side, a mug of milky tea, a Disney film playing on TV. I'm not jealous—well, maybe I am a bit—not of the cigarettes or the movie, but of the alone time, of the means to focus unapologetically on his art. I envy his lack of responsibility.

I rein in the leashes at the crosswalk, keeping Midge and Bets close to me. I can see the line of trees ahead and prepare for the mud. It rained heavily through the night. There is no avoiding it. I squeeze the last lungful of resentment out of my chest, steering the dogs to the left to bypass the deepest of puddles in the narrow alley that leads into the heart of the woods. Treading between weeds and stinging nettles, I acknowledge my part in the story. I brought Zach back to a country with an equally broken mental health care system, and to family that already has enough to deal with. Was it just a last-ditch measure on my part, yet again? Yes, I think, it probably was.

Under the canopy of oak trees, I let the dogs run free. The woody scent of the forest floor is thick after the downpour. The air is infused with negative ions. I can feel them start to calm my mind. Mike, my yoga teacher in Norfolk, told me how, unlike positive ions that are emitted through electronics, this negative source is created in nature by the effects of water, air, sunlight and the earth's radiation.

Bets mostly stays close to me. A bit older than Midge, she is well trained from her puppy classes. When Midge wanders too far, scurrying out of sight behind the trees, Betty, like a good scout leader, runs to fetch her, nudging her back toward me where she is safe.

"Thanks, Betty," I say.

I feel grounded by this ancient woodland. Here, for this short time, I look down at the trail and feel connected to the earth, what I have, who I am in the world.

This forest was permanently altered during Saxon times by something called pollarding—the selective cutting of trees. There is still evidence of it today, in trees that look misshapen. It is as if their limbs are too heavy for their trunks. I can't fathom how they can bear the weight. There are lots of fallen branches too: beech, birch, oak and hornbeam.

On the day before Nance is due to arrive, I ride the train then the bus to Dereham to visit Zach at his bed and breakfast. I am not sure how many more times I will be able to get to him before I leave for California, so I want every visit to count. I plan not to talk too much, just to be with him, to listen, to not argue.

We make our way to the local park. Zach unclips Midge from her leash and throws the ball high into the air for her. Of all the things he has lost passion for in life, Midge is not one of them. He adores her the way he did Belle and Suki and his cat Richard Parker, the way he loves all animals. I am grateful for this. It is no small feat. I wish he had his own dog so he wasn't so alone. Maybe one day, I tell myself, adding yet another thing to the hypothetical tally in my heart.

When I was a young girl and wished for things, mum used to have me stand out on the balcony of our high-rise apartment and look up into the night sky.

"Focus on a star. Say the rhyme, Tan," she encouraged. "It will come true if you believe it."

"Star light, star bright, the first star I see tonight. I wish I may, I wish I might, have this wish I wish tonight," I said, believing in the power of my words, and the star.

Mum was clever like that, able to bring a little nugget of magic from the heavens, just like Billy Bigelow in *Carousel*.

Nowadays, my wishes are tainted with ifs and buts and grown-up cynicism. What if Zach isn't allowed a dog where he is living? What if he sleeps too long and doesn't get the dog outside? What if he has to go into the hospital? What if he neglects the dog?

I watch him kick the ball backward onto the lawn. Midge dives on it like a goalkeeper. Zach's jeans are loose around his waist and slip down when he moves. I know that the weight loss comes from his being off his antipsychotic drugs. The hospital took him off the injectable to start the Clozaril, so at the moment he is off prescribed drugs completely.

"How long will you be gone for? Anything more than two weeks will be too long. I won't cope," he says. "Can I come back with you to America?"

It feels like a punch to my sternum when he asks this of me. I know that the USA is not a good place for Zach. I can't take him back and forth between two continents for the rest of time.

"Zach, you wanted to come here. I'll be back as soon as I can," I say, knowing how arbitrary it sounds.

As the sun is going down, he walks me to the bus stop.

"We can Skype, Zigs. I'm just on the other end of the phone, okay?"

I hug him tight and go to plant a kiss on his cheek. He turns his head down so it lands on his crown. I feel thankful, remembering the times he wouldn't allow me to hug or kiss him at all. It is raining hard by the time the bus arrives. I grab a seat on the lower deck close to the heating vents. The darkening sky and the wet weather make it hard for me to see out of the window, but I think I see him duck into the fish and chip shop. I am relieved he is eating, although a part of me wishes he would eat more healthily. Serotonin levels in the gut have been found to be deficient in people experiencing psychosis and major depression. Vitamin D levels are often compromised too. Gut health is being deemed more and more crucial as a way of improving brain function. It makes sense, given the mind–body connection.

I have other wishes, aside from the dietary issues. I wish Zach had a friend. I wish Gordon were more invested in him. I wish he had safe, supported housing. I wish I could clone myself, leave one of me here. I wish my mum wasn't dead. I wish we could start again, from the night in the laundry room, or the day we got on the plane to Los Angeles, or the early hours of the morning that Zach was born.

I try to look up into the night sky, but the ceiling of the bus blocks my vision. I know it is too early to see the stars yet. I say the rhyme anyway, holding on to Midge as we pull away, allowing her to keep me steady. It is almost a year ago that I rescued her, and, in turn, she has saved me countless times.

Back in London with Janey and Jo, I check my flight app before I go to sleep. Nance's plane is right on schedule. She is above Canada, making her way to me.

The next morning, I am still downsizing, wondering what I should do with Midge's cumbersome crate, when Nance texts me. She is here in London. We will be staying in Room 285 at the Langham on Portland Place, a fancy old Victorian hotel in the West End.

I try to lessen my load so I can manage on the tube. I have too

many dresses, books, dog toys. When I climb out of the under-
ground onto Regent Street, I am both thrilled and apprehensive
about seeing Nance again. This war of sorts has distanced us for
so long. People have done this throughout history, though. Soldiers
leave for battle. Refugees and immigrants get separated for years at
a time. They survive. They reunite. Absence makes the heart grow
fonder, I tell myself. I think about all the years that Nance worked
in the bay area while I stayed in LA. We might not have survived the
fallout of Zach's experiences of psychosis without retreating to our
individual refuges in the storm.

"We're getting close now, Midge—you'll get to see Mama 2," I
say. The scruffy little dog wags and pulls on the leash.

I want to use the hotel's side entrance, but I don't have a keycard
to gain access. With Midge in tow, and my possessions stuffed into
a rucksack, I look like I belong at the Travelodge for £29.99 a night.
Instead, I am about to step into the grand foyer of five-star luxury
accommodation where breakfast alone costs £38.

I brace myself, hoist Midge under one arm and push against
the revolving door that leads into the lobby. I move quickly across
the Victorian floor tiles into the architectural beauty of the Regent
Wing and call the lift. On the way up, I think about Zach in his
little hovel of a room.

I step out of the hotel elevator onto a plush runner. Black and
white framed photographs showing a bygone Portland Place line the
hallways.

I am here. Room 285. I feel giddy, like a lovestruck teenager, as I
knock on the door.

Nance answers, her earbuds in and her phone raised in one hand.
She is on a call. She beams at me and holds one finger in the air to

indicate she is almost done. She looks thinner and alert, despite having flown for ten hours.

I rush Midge into the bathroom. She struggles as I wash her paws with the luxury hotel soap. Nance, forever adept at multitasking, places a blanket on top of the bed for her.

She finishes her call and turns to me. "How are you doing?" she asks.

"I'm good," I say, moving in to embrace her. "You look great. Do you not feel jet-lagged?"

"Not yet," she says.

I exclaim how great it is to be here, how lovely the room is. Then I get down to business. "I'm so hungry," I confess. "Shall we get Honest Burgers for late lunch?"

"Sure. I have a couple more calls to make, then I'm free."

"I'll grab them if you can watch Midge?" I offer. It feels like old times already—the compromises, the sharing, the excitement of vegan food and togetherness.

"I have photos to show you," she says.

I love her pictures. She has such a flair for capturing the creatures and the landscape. I smile.

"I'm here, honey. I'm really here." I hug her again, grab my purse and head out.

"Get me fries and no bun," she shouts after me.

Back at the hotel, I realize I have bought much more food for me than for Nance, yet out of habit I still steal a few of her fries.

We eat, then lie together in the center of the enormous bed. Nance clicks through photos of our rescued cat Donna climbing trees on the property. Richard Parker, Zach's cat, with his emerald eyes, looks as grumpy as ever. I wonder if he misses Zach, his close buddy for almost seven years.

Nance reaches for the TV remote, which she has placed in a

little plastic bag in case it harbors germs. She thinks of everything, even flip-flops to wear in the shower. We watch some TV, a travel program, and I place my head on her chest. I have truly missed her. When we come to the end of the show, she grows serious.

"If it's going to be too hard for you to come home just yet, I get it. We will survive this. I'm not going anywhere, Tan," she says.

Her doubt that I might not come back with her after all makes me question my intention and clouds my resolve. What if this recent separation has created an emotional distance that can never be bridged, despite a few minutes of looking at photographs? What if absence has torn our hearts apart?

I want to get close to her again, but the anonymity of Regent Street and this lonely, transient capital city winds its way up to the second floor. It sneaks under the door, into our room and under the quilt of the king-size bed. I feel its stranglehold. Nance shuts the laptop.

"I feel so tired now. I think the jet lag has finally caught up with me," she says. She turns over, reaching behind her to pat my thigh.

We used to snuggle, to cuddle, to spoon, to throw arms and legs around each other, to warm cold feet, but I don't know how to touch her anymore. She even sleeps in a way that I cannot intrude upon, connected to her phone, with the quilt tucked tightly around her.

She falls asleep quickly. I am about to follow suit when Zach calls. The ring is jarring. I place the phone under the covers to muffle the sound, but I feel Nance move next to me.

Zach is nocturnal again, but in surprisingly high spirits. He is rapping, which feels torturous at this late hour. I catch some of it. Something about Midge and a bridge and the mother-fucking bitch. "That's good, Zach," I feign, wondering if I should mention the swearing, "but it is so late. Nance is asleep."

"There is more to it," he says. "Wait."

I lower the volume and give him a few more seconds, then I tell him I need to sleep, and end the call.

I cannot turn off. I look at Nance, her small head on the pillow. The sadness of losing her mum seems evident, even at rest. I know what it is to lose one's mother. I want to help. I want to be there for her. I'm relieved I'll be going back with her. Even if it is hard for her to talk right now, I'll be with her in the flesh through all her grief.

In the morning I am still tired and heavy from last night's big supper as I perch on the bed and sip my coffee. Nance has already been out running in Regent's Park, and she smells good after showering. She is getting ready for work.

"Do you think me coming home might be too much for you?" I ask her, trying to keep my tone unemotional. "The fact that the cabin is so small, and you are used to your own space there now?"

"Well, if you can maybe go downstairs to talk to Zach, if he calls you during the night," she says, "so it doesn't disturb me."

I have woken her so many nights by picking up the phone to Zach. I would sit on the toilet in the bathroom, the only room with a door in our tiny cabin, trying to keep my voice down as I watched the spiders that dwelled in the upper reaches of the stall. Will it even feel like home anymore?

Nance is consumed by work in the coming days, trying to cancel travel plans for clients flying to the USA from Japan, where something called coronavirus is spreading. Two nights in a row she stays on the phone until midnight. The stress is visible in her shoulders, which I rub a little bit, not sure if I am really helping.

How nice it might be if we could go out for dinner, but Nance doesn't do dinner anymore, she tells me. I say that a big lunch sounds very healthy, and I'd like to try to do the same, but underneath I am hungry. I am starving. It is all I can think about. I feel so empty.

Nance has Hashimoto's, a condition that affects the thyroid. She manages it by avoiding all foods that cause inflammation, such as gluten, soy and dairy. A year ago, she gave up alcohol. I love her and her discipline, I really do, but I wish we could have dinner and cocktails and do something, anything, other than work and worry. It is hard for me to let go of Zach. Nance relies on work. We both have our crutches this way.

"I'm finally done," Nance says one evening as the week draws to a close. "I think things will calm down a bit with work now."

She gives my arm a rub. I love this brief physical exchange. It reminds me of how things used to be, and how they might be again one day when we are all settled, when Nance is retired, and we are able to find a country home in the UK. We have spoken about the idea a few times now. Our dream of Nance relocating to England. I know as much as I've ever known that Zach needs me on the same continent. Maybe it is my own need too, to acknowledge that I cannot walk away forever.

Some nights, Nance watches Midge while I swim in the infinity pool on the ground floor. Afterward, in the shower under a strong jet of steamy hot water, I allow myself to cry. I fear losing Nance. I worry I have already lost a part of Zach. Nance has lost her mum. I am scared I might lose myself, my mind. Life feels so much about loss.

"How was it?" Nance asks when I return to the room.

"It was great," I say, "really great."

I hear from the owner of the temporary accommodation where Zach is staying. He is not letting anyone in to clean the room. He doesn't allow anyone from his mental health team to enter his space either. They can't get through to him on the phone and he hasn't responded to their letters.

Zach's social worker will eventually want to discharge him from services because of his unwillingness to engage, as she puts it, but for now a multidisciplinary meeting has been arranged for Monday morning. I am asked if I can attend and help Zach to get there. The meeting is important because it might help us to get the right level of care and support in terms of accommodation. However, Nance and I have arranged to spend a long weekend in the bohemian town of Hebden Bridge in Yorkshire, a place claimed by hippies, lesbians and alternative thinkers. We are excited.

We have planned to make our leisurely way back to London on Monday. To make the meeting I would have to leave on the 5:30 a.m. train. I ask the team to change the date, but they say it is impossible. I cannot assume that Zach will wake up early. He rarely rises before late afternoon. I ask Gordon to support him, but he still has his chest infection. His sister refuses to help. I don't want to admit it but in some way it makes sense that she isn't available. Gordon and his sister, Marcia, have had seventeen years of a life that hasn't revolved around Zach. Why then would she drive to Dereham, attempt to wake him up, cajole him into her car and commute thirty miles to meet with people that he does not trust or wish to talk to, all while I am on holiday with my wife?

I don't tell Nance. Holding this secret inside feels as if it might tear me in two. Nance/Zach, Zach/Nance.

On the day before we leave for Yorkshire, I order breakfast for us both. It is delivered to our room on a cart with a white tablecloth draped over it. There is toast (gluten free, which Nance doesn't eat just in case it isn't truly gluten free), vegan sausages (that again she doesn't quite trust), and eggs, scrambled, which she does eat, despite the fact they may have a little butter in them. She has tomato juice, too, and some tea. The hash browns might have some wheat in them, you never know, so she resists those too. I eat everything, including the items that Nance leaves, and stare quietly at the pink fragrant rose that sits in a white vase next to the marmalade.

"I think it will be easier once I get back to the cabin again," I tell her, "I really do."

"I'm worried you will just be so anxious, if you come home," she says, knowing me well after so long. "You're bad enough now when you don't hear from Zach for a day. What will you be like from over five thousand miles away?"

I feel queasy, trying to imagine how I will be. "I'll just have to manage," I tell her. I promise more therapy, more effort to become independent, and to let Zach do the same.

Nance has lost weight since I left and stopped cooking big suppers. She has cut her hair short, dyed it a shiny chestnut brown. It suits her. She looks younger, cuter than she has in years. Clothes from Muji, Zara, Urban Outfitters hang neatly in the hotel closet, and four pairs of shoes line up against the wall. In her open suitcase, socks stay with socks in a zippered bag. Panties with panties. Toiletries together.

I, on the other hand, have not been taking care of myself. My hair hasn't been dyed since I left California. I have put on weight. Nance explains lovingly that she is worried about me, that she has never seen me this big, and knows I have cancer in my family. Being overweight is linked to certain kinds of cancer.

I weigh myself in the hotel bathroom. What Nance says is true. My frustration and feelings of failure have led me to seek solace in carbs. I eat standing up. I eat food straight out of the frying pan. I eat walking around the supermarket. I eat my feelings, every single last one of them.

After Nance leaves for work, I take Midge to Regent's Park. It is muddy from the recent rainfall, and I don't have my boots. I wander along the side of the pond, trying to stop Midge from chasing the ducks. It is a tad chilly, but I realize despite the hardship that I am quite smitten with London. It is as if I am a foreigner. Everything is novel. I am falling back in love with the land of my birth, my youth, my past, and this capital city I had forsaken. I am a stranger, and I am alone, yet a part of me is very much at home, comforted by being outside, moving in time with my breath.

Out of habit, I try to reach Zach. His phone goes straight to voicemail. I hope he hasn't seen the news about the virus. This is not the time for more worry. I put my phone in my back pocket and wonder if I will always want to know where and how Zach is, for the rest of my life.

15

YORKSHIRE

I place my hand on Nance's thigh, and feel her leg muscles grow taut when she depresses the clutch to change gear.

"Just look at that view," she says, slowing on a country lane to take a picture. The rain of late has cast everything a dewy green.

"If we do retire to this area, I'd like a house like that one in the middle of that field. It has to have those old stone walls around it," I insist.

"Yes, definitely an old farmhouse," she answers. "Not too far from the nearest town or village. Something that needs renovating, so it's affordable."

These are the conversations that bring us close. I want to ask if Zach can live with us too, but it is too early in the day, too soon in the trip. I don't want to compromise our time together by putting Nance on the spot. It can wait.

Before we drive up to the converted barn that we have rented for the weekend, we stop off at the high street in Hebden Bridge to browse the local shops. We find organic farm produce at the health food co-operative, and Nance is thrilled to buy a beautiful, fresh loaf of gluten-free bread from the bakery. Everyone is friendly. We could live here.

Early the next morning we hike to Hardcastle Crags, taking the upper trail through the woodland after the locals tell us to avoid the route that crosses the recently flooded River Calder. The morning light streams through the conifers. We pass through the town of Midge Hole, giggling because we know instantly that our poor dog will now have a new nickname. A couple of miles in, the trail descends and we see the river, swollen, loud and rushing.

I remember a time when Zach loved to ramble with us, with Nance especially. It was before they began to pull apart—two objects of like charge repelling each other with magnetic force. There was one hike in particular, along a watery force of nature like this one, named Switzer Falls. We frequented it so often that in the end we just called it Switzers.

Switzers was an oasis in the high desert of the Arroyo Seco. The day that we brought Dale and Zach there, the snowfall on the San Gabriels had been plentiful, and the ice melt amplified the waterfall and filled the lower pool. What few people knew was that by crossing the water and scrambling up around the boulders, it was possible to get above the waterfall.

We showed the boys the way. Above the falls was an upper pool, but higher still was where the real magic lay hidden: a natural playground. A smooth channel carved in the rock had created a magnificently perfect slide. Dale and Zach, already throwing off their shoes and t-shirts, could ride a chute and plunge into water so frigid it would take their breath away.

"Scream out once you surface," I told them. We couldn't see the upper pool from where we stood, but I trusted that their strong voices would carry inside the canyon walls.

Dale went first, sliding down the channel with ease. "Woo-hoo," we heard him shout. Once he clambered back up the rock, Zach took off. He raised his arms into the air and then disappeared. I strained to hear him. Nothing.

I listened again, harder. Then I panicked.

"Zach," I screamed, my voice bouncing off the granite in a cruel echo.

"He's okay," said Nance, always the calm optimist.

"He's not okay," I yelled. "He's not okay." I imagined him cracking his head on a rock on the way down, being pulled under by an eddy in the water and toppling into the lower pool. Nance began to edge down to see if she could see him, and I waited, frozen, realizing we had no cell service. I imagined Nance running to her car, driving to the ranger's station, summoning a helicopter that would be forced to hover above the craggy rocks to rescue Zach. A sickening sense of doom overwhelmed me.

"He's okay," Nance shouted, after spotting him climbing out of the pool.

He clambered back up the rocks on all fours. "That was so cool, I want to do it again," he said, his smile enormous, his curly brown hair dripping icy cold water all over us.

"See, you worry too much, Tan," said Nance. "Just shout out for your mum's sake, Zach—you know what she's like."

On our way home, as we weaved along the Los Angeles Crest Highway, Dale and Zach fell asleep in the back seat.

"He's not okay. He's not okay," Nance piped up out of the blue, impersonating my high-pitched voice. I laughed. *He's not okay* became a family joke that only we found funny, until it wasn't anymore.

Our hidden forest jewel would stop being okay too. Graffiti would taint the rocks at our precious Switzers, sand and silt would fill the pools, and beer cans would litter the ground. Droughts would diminish the waterfall, and one of the worst forest fires in recent history would spread poodle-dog bush, which causes a poison-oak-like rash in sensitive people. But this wouldn't be the Switzers I would recall. Mine would be forever idyllic, a cathedral of white canyon walls arching over the baptisms we performed in our own bohemian way.

We are divided now, no longer together as a family in this ancient Yorkshire woodland with its citrusy scent of pine. Yet Nance has come alive as she navigates the trail, and I feel rejuvenated too. I hold her hand. We do not talk about Zach. We barely talk at all. We breathe deeply and laugh as Midge picks up sticks. We cross the stream at Gibson Mill, an English Heritage site with a café that sells tea and homemade cakes.

I like it here, where lesbians in Doc Martens and scruffy terriers like Midge seem to abound. I'm drawn toward the alternative vibe. I consider again how we might all benefit from living somewhere more tolerant of difference.

In the afternoon, as we are on our way to Haworth, I tell Nance about the meeting for Zach.

"Maybe I can drive down with you?" she offers.

"Really?" I ask, thinking about how Nance has been able to let go of the desperate desire to fix Zach, yet still helps with the practicalities. Maybe I can let go of the logistics and enjoy the rest of the trip?

Our last stop before returning to our accommodation is a detour to a farmhouse that we saw advertised online. We want to get an idea of sale prices for when the time is right. It starts to rain. We weave our way back and forth on the dirt roads, but we cannot find the property anywhere. Suddenly Nance points at the sky, where a faint black shadow, like metal filings on an old Etch A Sketch screen, begins to swarm. We stop the car and get out to watch.

"I think it's a murmuration," Nance says. "Starlings."

The birds dip and dive, a great whoosh of energy and life. High above them, we spot a solitary bird of prey, a sparrowhawk or peregrine falcon.

"You know that was on my bucket list?" I say as we climb back into the car. Nance nods. The birds have gone, but the spell has been cast. Not being able to locate the farmhouse no longer matters.

We are pulling back onto the main road when I say, "This place is so special, do you think Zach could live with us, if we find a piece of land big enough? Not right on top of us, but maybe in a cabin or an outbuilding?"

"I don't know, Tan."

A part of me understands. I think back to the times when Zach stopped the medicine cold turkey, broke things, slid his fist through walls, doors, my car windscreen. He left phones and consoles on the street, my laptop on the front doorstep, so "they" couldn't track him. I don't blame him, and I don't talk about it much, and it might not happen again. But these are facts that create in me the kind of grief that makes me weep.

"It sure is beautiful here," Nance says the next morning as we leave the Calder Valley. "I'm too raw to make any decision about buying somewhere right now though." Her eyes look watery. I wish I could comfort her. I know how grief burrows like a foxtail seed. This plant, native to California, can penetrate the skin and travel deep into the body. But these tiny moments, these slivers of pain that she holds out for me to see, are so brief.

The drive to Norfolk is long and tiring. We take the wrong roads and almost run out of petrol. Eventually I realize there is no way I will make it on time, so I call to say that Zach and I will not be able to attend the meeting.

I still visit him anyway, alone, taking over the rental car. Nance returns to London by train.

16

CRANWORTH

It is a brief visit with Zach. I am exhausted, cross at the world, trying to fit in too many things. I am angry that Zach could not wake up and get to the meeting on his own, that Nance and I had to cut our trip short, that Gordon was sick.

I hold Midge tightly and sit on Zach's bed in the shabby accommodation. The sheets are dirty, the towels are damp.

I notice his phone on the side, next to the sink unit with the bare chipboard and the missing Formica. "You can call your dad if you need to talk," I tell him. "You have your team, too. Just rely on them. I won't be gone too long."

He closes his eyes. "My bank card has gone missing," he says, almost too dejected to spit out the words. "Things keep being moved around in here."

"It's probably me," I say, even though I haven't been there for a few days. I just don't want him to worry. For a moment I stop talking. I have said so much already. Zach is quiet and stares at his hands, really examining them. Then he grabs one of my hands and compares it in size to his own. He draws the curtains more fully. The only sound is that of a few patrons chatting in the garden, and the solitary squawk of a crow. I am not sure what to say to Zach other than I love you, and goodbye, yet again.

I look at his guitar growing dusty in the corner of the room and remember how they jammed—he and Dale—for hours, doing something they called minor pentatonic scales. It just seemed to work, the way they picked and plucked at the strings. Perhaps everything will find its own rhythm in the end, like the harmonies the boys put together on those instruments. My sister Zoë knew intuitively how to manage her own affairs once she had to. It was after mum died when she found herself through the grieving process. Maybe the same thing will happen to Zach when I leave the country. Perhaps Gordon will take up the slack. The community mental health team will see that Zach is completely alone and may take his plight more seriously.

I can't be indispensable. I will die one day, like everyone else.

I let Midge down onto the bed, watch her burrow under Zach's arm, lick his nose, push his face up to the light.

I am about to use the bathroom before leaving when I notice it—a hole the size of a fist in the bathroom door. A new one that looks like the others that were already here when Zach moved in.

"Oh no. What the fuck?" I say.

Zach looks at his fist, which is still red from the incident. He mutters something about the voices making him do it, driving him to despair.

This is probably why so many of the other young men who lived in this room before him, full of rage and frustration at the hand they had been dealt, punched holes in the doors too, and why the bed and breakfast manager gave up trying to prettify the accommodation long ago.

"You'll have to pay for those damages out of your benefit," I say.

It is on this note that I leave Dereham, not wanting to depart any more than I wanted to stay, caught as always between love and resentment, sorrow about the past and fear of the future. What I don't see in myself is how I am moving ever so gradually into a new formation, a dance I don't quite yet understand because I haven't learned all the moves.

My partners are out there, though—my group, my groove. I must seek them out so I can find a way to rise as well as fall, to swoop but not crash, to sleep on the wing, to keep flying.

It is late when I reach the Langham. The image of Zach in his room has traveled back with me, and I feel torn. I have one last day to make up my mind about whether to stay here or leave for America. The next morning, I am still deciding what to do in a push and pull tug of war.

Nance should already have left for work, but she comes out of the bathroom looking troubled. It is possible she knows more than I do about this coronavirus thing. She wears earbuds to go to sleep and has the news drifting into her subconscious. Maybe the meetings at work have prepped her for how bad this is going to be. I stop and take stock.

She approaches me and buries her head in my neck and starts to cry. It is a gentle sob to begin with, but it builds. I weep too, realizing by the way she is holding me that it is about us, our situation. The two of us stand in the middle of the hotel room, unable to let each other go. Because I have so rarely seen Nance cry, it is shocking. There was the time she wept shortly after Zach was first diagnosed. She met him on the stairs to the basement and told him she was sorry, and I heard her choke back tears. She cried when her father lay dying and she had to rise every few hours to drip morphine under his tongue, then again when I found her locked in her car on the farm in Los Gatos. And now she cries once more. As much as it unnerves me to see her in this state, I try to find solace in the fact that it is a release.

She lets go of me. In an instant she is composed again, back to her buttoned-up self. "I don't want this to influence you," she says. "I don't want this to make your decision for you. I'll be okay if you have to stay here. I will," she says.

She goes to the bathroom and fixes her eye make-up, and then with a brief wave, she leaves for work. Sometimes Nance strikes me as more English than me—her stiff upper lip and tight rein on her emotions—until, like now, her feelings rise unexpectedly, like a flash flood in a canyon.

It is mid-afternoon when my phone rings. It is the assessments manager from Together UK, a network of residential and supported living homes in West Norfolk that I had reached out to weeks ago. The manager informs me that she has spoken to her intake team, and that if I am able to self-pay for Zach, he can live in one of the apartments. I need to provide them with some paperwork and visit with Zach to make sure that it is a good fit. I ask if we can move quickly, given the fact that I want to get back to California as soon as possible.

She thinks we can.

I hang up and envisage Midge and I getting on a plane once Zach is settled and safe, with round-the-clock staff to support him. I will finally be able to take a break. The head office is going to crunch the numbers for me and will be back in touch. It is this phone call that clinches the deal, affecting my decision not to leave with Nance, but rather to stay in the UK with Zach until he has moved into his new accommodation.

I lie on the plump mattress of the hotel bed and close my eyes. I imagine being back in California with the elephant seals. I have missed the birthing season. The weaners will be getting ready to take their first voyage, splashing in the pools and inlets left after high tide. I think about their mothers, how easily they left their pups once they had weaned them, how they are free of all maternal responsibility now, swimming in the deep pelagic waters. They have done their job. Soon it will start all over again. These females already have embryos waiting to implant in the walls of their wombs. The fertilized eggs won't attach until the female seals have had a chance to forage and get fat again—this is called delayed implantation. The adult male elephant seals will have left Año too, swimming closer to the coastline, seeking out a different diet. Their migratory route is longer, more dangerous, as they travel in more heavily shark-infested waters.

That night, I wake up to a text from a friend in California who says that I need to check the status of flights heading back to the USA from Europe. She believes that Trump has closed the borders. I shake Nance awake and tell her.

"No!" she screams out, and I think I might see her cry for the fifth time in our seventeen-year union.

We look at the news online. Trump has indeed banned all incoming flights from Europe, but the USA is still open to its citizens and residents returning home from the UK. Nance is visibly relieved, but I am nervous. What if things change and I get stuck here?

Her outburst leaves me unsettled. Is she scared to stay in England with its poor overstretched NHS, or does she just need to get back for work, for the cats? I know instinctively that life in the Santa Cruz Mountains, on our very affluent and sparsely populated road, will be a safer place than here during a pandemic. I also know that the grass is always greener on the other side. Growing up in London, I yearned for the chance to live with Auntie Betty in America. Once settled into the Hollywood house on the crest of the hill, I grew homesick for family and friends and the life I had left behind in

London. I feel myself craning my neck, looking out across the pond, ready to run away again.

Nance wakes early. She packed her case last night, but she wants to do a final check. She is hyper-focused on getting out on time.

"I'm not sure where to stay," I tell her. "I think I should be as close to Zach as possible."

"Norwich might be a good place—you can get the bus from there to go and see him. You liked it there," she reminds me.

I nod. I can't fit everything in the new travel bag I bought on Regent Street, so Nance repacks it for me, rolling things up Marie Kondo-style and putting some of my excess attire in her suitcase to take back with her. I feel like I want her to bundle me up too, make me inanimate so I don't have to feel pain, or make difficult decisions.

The cab that will transport Nance to Heathrow is waiting just outside. She pops her luggage in the trunk and hugs me briefly. There are no tears this time. I wait with Midge until the car pulls away, and I wave. The windows of the vehicle are tinted. I cannot see her. I feel cheated.

Back upstairs, I look at various places to stay in Norfolk. I try Dereham on Airbnb, but all I can find is a room in a shared house with a doctor.

Eventually I find a little cottage in a village called Cranworth, which lies about six miles south of Dereham in the countryside. It has every facility that I require and will allow me to check in tonight. The owner lives in the main farmhouse adjoining the property. Her proximity is not ideal—I'd like to have some space and privacy in case Zach wants to stay. But I am getting quite anxious trying to find something at this point. The reviews are favorable and the owner is a designated Superhost. She makes fresh soda bread for her guests. I am sold.

I board the train at King's Cross. Midge settles on the empty seat next to me on her thin, soft blanket. Two guys adjacent to me are discussing the coronavirus. They are medical students or personnel, or it seems that way from their conversation. They are belaboring the fact that so little is known about this new strain of respiratory illness. One of the young men lifts his scarf and coughs into it, and I feel myself shrink away, edging closer to the window. Another passenger in the seat opposite me is on the phone and tells whoever is on the other end that she isn't feeling well at all.

"I have a temperature, I think, and a sore throat," she says.

There is nowhere else for me to move to. The train is full. I lift the pashmina I am wearing to conceal my mouth and nose. I wonder if I am being overly cautious.

I keep myself hidden behind the fabric until the train pulls into King's Lynn.

There are no buses that serve Cranworth, so I rent a car. I do a double take at the large white SUV.

"This is the only car the company has left," the driver says. "You can have it at the same price."

It reminds me of America—the worst of America—a gas-guzzling monstrosity. Still, I take it. I drive away with the duffel and Midge in the rear, while my sense of uncertainty hitches a ride up front, clawing at my chest.

I stop off at Zach's. He has the radiators turned up full blast, despite it being a gloriously warm spring evening. It smells stale, so I open the window. He is lying in bed with the sheet twisted around him. He always seems to be supine these days—horizontal but not restful, not at peace. He still sleeps with his shoes and jeans on. His right arm is propped under his head. I notice how his bicep looks weak and atrophied from lack of exercise.

The room was rather squalid to begin with, but now it is decidedly more so with dirty clothes, left-over food and general disarray. The carpet is filthy. I start to clean, out of habit and fear. I'm worried that Zach could be evicted before he is able to move into the supported living accommodation. This must be avoided at all costs, even if it means me scooping out remnants of Pot Noodle from the sink. I think about how I promised Nance many years ago that I wouldn't clean up after Zach. Am I regressing? Do I not have the means to learn from the past? How many days or weeks might it take, I wonder, for Zach to clean up after himself if I just left him, left it?

Raising his head off the pillow, the furrow between his brows looks far too deep for someone his age.

"I decided to stay here for a couple more weeks," I tell him. "I want to talk to you about moving into a new flat, somewhere safer. Not that it isn't safe here or anything, but a place with more support. Somewhere with staff who can help you clean up."

Zach asks me to slow down and just tell him one piece of information at a time. He then accuses me of doublespeak, which sounds oddly Orwellian, but I think it means that he is hearing the voices in his head as well as my voice, and it gets confusing to try to decode who is saying what.

He blinks a few times. "You came back," he mutters. "Nice."

This is as close as I am going to get to a thank you, so I accept it.

"What is this coronavirus hoax?" he asks.

I realize he must have seen something on the news.

"What do you mean?"

"I mean, it's bullcrap."

"I wish you were right, Zigs," I say, following NHS protocol and washing my hands for as long as it takes me to sing happy birthday twice over in my head.

"I've rented a place in a village just south of here. Let me check it out. It's meant to have a sofabed. Maybe you can stay over one night if you want to?"

"Sure," Zach agrees, then as if he has forgotten or not heard me at all, he accompanies me to the car and tries to come with me.

"No, Zach," I assert, even though I know he feels unsafe here, targeted and talked about. "I need to see what it's like first."

It is dark by the time I leave Dereham. Other than large patches of blackness that cloak either side of the lane, I can't see much of the surrounding landscape, just shadowy outlines of trees in the distance.

It isn't easy to get to sleep in the cottage. I calculate the number of homes and hotels I have slept in since coming back to England, and the fact I am becoming increasingly nomadic. Each day I wake to the uncanny sense of not knowing for a moment or two where I am. I wonder if this is what Zach lives with most of the time, and how it must feel to have been left so often by so many people.

Although Gordon upped and went, he didn't disappear forever the way my father did. We knew where Gordon was. We also knew he went on to marry, to have two more children with his new wife.

Dale dressed in black during this period. He used the same color to paint and draw pictures at nursery school. He asked his teachers to call him Gordon. It was as if he was in mourning. Zach seemed untouched by the experience.

"Maybe he's too young to understand," I recall saying to my mum. "He seems fine."

Zach had learned to say "dada" in the months before Gordon left, and on the nights that Dale went to bed early, Gordon bounced Zach on his knee and sang, "To market to market to buy a fat pig," or "Ride a cock horse to Banbury Cross." Sometimes the two of them played Tickle Monster. The rules were simple: Gordon raised his arms in the air as if he might tickle Zach's armpits, tummy, under his chin. Zach squealed in anticipation, but rarely was there any contact.

As I lie here, just me, in this new place, I can't help but think about Zach just a few miles north of me, and how he doesn't want to be alone. Gordon is on his own now too, just a bit farther inland; Dale is the only person from our family in the USA right now. Nance is flying solo over the Atlantic.

Was Zach truly too young to understand that his father left? Is there ever a perfect age to say goodbye to your father and watch him form a new life?

After we separated, when Gordon came to take the boys out for a few hours every Sunday, Dale was always ready to go. He was the one who sometimes cried upon coming home. He also cried when he wasn't invited to go on holiday with Gordon and his new family. Zach, on the other hand, tottered in and out of the mix with less angst—or at least it seemed that way. He had never appeared to need his father desperately the way that Dale did, to want him, to crave his attention and his affection. Not until now, but now is not good timing. Gordon's daughter needs him just as much. She is younger and the only girl, and in some ways it is hard for me to comprehend that she still comes first.

There is so much that Gordon and Zach have in common. They both like tea, milky coffee with sugar, biscuits, sausage and chips, Disney films, roll-up cigarettes. They are both history buffs. But it isn't enough. Not for me. I want more for Zach. When Gordon says "son of mine," I want Zach to feel a sense of total belonging, a secure knowledge that even if his moods and fears and extreme states cause pain, he can be accommodated, understood, held completely, without anything or anyone else getting in the way.

1 7

PULLED OVER

I walk and walk and walk. Midge looks back at me and picks up a stick, teasing it between her jaws, pulling on the leash. The lanes here are narrow, unpaved, but it doesn't matter, as the only traffic is a solitary tractor. I pass an alpaca farm, which reminds me of Frank and Omer on the mountain in Los Gatos. Whether it is the wilds of Año Nuevo or here, within the old parish of St. Mary, that dates to the fourteenth century, the great outdoors is such a balm for a sore mind and sagging spirit. No wonder that doctors on the NHS are now starting to prescribe nature bathing.

I see no signs of working village life in Cranworth. The post office has become a dwelling, the only clue to its origins an old red post box in the front garden. The local library and the chapel have been converted, too. Built, as the plaque confirms, in 1838, the chapel has a simple brick façade and ornate arch windows. Inside, there is a spiral staircase and an old stone hearth. It looks like a haven for the family that lives there.

On my way to Southburgh I come across a smokehouse for fish. The placard on the lane advertises the recent catch: two fillets of cod for a fiver. I am more and more convinced that it will help Zach to spend the odd night here with me while we wait for his supported accommodation. We can turn his body clock around—walk in the mornings, eat fresh fish for dinner.

I keep going, oblivious of time. The only sound, other than the rustling of leaves, is the occasional loud pop of a bird-scarer installed by the farmers. The noise blights the landscape, reminds me of gun-shots, beagles, bugles, men on horseback. Hunting is still allowed here, with permits. It seems so archaic, so wrong. Zach is hunted, in a way. The derogatory voices—despite coming from within—make him feel cornered and trapped. I track him down, too, when I am scared, as do the police and his mental health team, often at my insistence.

Midge is all motion now, excited by the Norfolk wind that has suddenly whipped up, keen to get to the local field where I can let her run freely. I should probably stick to the public footpath that snakes around the perimeter, but Midge has other ideas. I untether her. She darts in and out of the fallow dirt and makes me laugh.

If only I could unclip Zach from the reins of his suffering as eas-ily as undoing a metal clasp on a dog leash. I ponder how it must be for him not to read, not to write; no computer, no job, no car, no intimate partner, just one person to rely on for all his needs—me. It is no wonder that he is often unable to put one foot in front of the other, that he lies down on the spot wherever he is, because being human and upright is unbearable.

"Tan, you can't possibly know how Zach feels, and you shouldn't even try to second guess," my friend Janey warns me. Is she right?

Back at the entrance to Holly Farm, I savor a few more moments before heading inside. A cloud floats into my orbit, backlit by the sun, its edges glowing with promise. I try to focus on the times that still shine, the occasions I see Zach smile or do a silly dance in the middle of Morrisons. Inside the cottage, my blood is reoxygenated. I call the manager of Together UK to ask if she has had a chance to talk to the team, and when Zach and I might be able to visit the premises. She tells me the staff member she wanted me to meet has had to take early maternity leave.

"Can you hold on for just a few more days? I can get you the figures for self-pay and find out what we need in the way of paperwork," she says.

"Sure," I say, but I feel let down. I think about Trump closing the border, the airlines canceling flights, the risks of flying and catching the virus. A few days seem like an infinitely long time.

After lunch I make my way to Dereham to pick up Zach and his washing. As I drive past the chapel my phone rings. Zach's social worker informs me that she has sent a letter to Zach to say that if he does not engage with his team, they will be forced to discharge him from services. I try to explain that his lack of interaction results from fear and trauma, and ask whether anyone there can spend time with him, even in silence. She reiterates the fact that under the Mental Health Act, Zach is within his rights to refuse services if he is deemed to have capacity. When I try to press my case, she reminds me that due to privacy laws she is unable to discuss the particulars any further without Zach's permission.

I want to scream. I know his team is overworked and under-resourced, and that Zach is considered a difficult case. He is classed as having anosognosia—a clinical term describing a lack of insight into his difficulties. He is also seen as noncompliant—which is how the biomedical model describes people who refuse antipsychotic drugs, even if the side effects wreak havoc on their minds and bodies.

I think back to Zach's hospital stay in King's Lynn and how the ward turned him away once he had refused the clozapine trial. Now his community mental health team want to discharge him, and I feel that I am once again alone and grappling with the fact that if Together UK doesn't accept Zach, or if Zach doesn't accept Together UK, we will be in a similar position to the one we were in last year, and all the years before that. The only difference is that now we are on the other side of the ocean, and completely alone.

I reach the King's Head and nip into the hotel to speak to the manager.

"I didn't get on the plane," I say.

"That's good, because the hotel may close."

"The block where Zach is housed, too?" I ask.

"No, just the communal areas."

Zach doesn't take advantage of these. He is entitled to a cooked breakfast four mornings a week, but even if he were awake on time he would no doubt be too suspicious to eat the chef's food. He doesn't visit the bar either. But the manager and her assistant being here during the day offers a degree of safety, at least for me. Knowing there is someone I can call from ten in the morning until eleven at night gives me some peace of mind.

"We probably won't close for a while," she says. "London will be the first to go into lockdown, I imagine."

I know she is trying to reassure me, but the idea that Zach will be alone here without anyone onsite, and with the possibility that he will be discharged from services, makes me bite my lip.

"I'll still come in to check up on the vulnerable guests," she adds. "Mondays, Wednesdays and Fridays at 10 a.m. The only problem is that Zach doesn't open his door to me. The cleaning staff haven't been able to get in for ages."

"I know, I am so sorry. I'll speak to him again," I say. I want to tell her that Zach is fearful of the purple toilet bleach, and probably the cleaning staff too, but I don't know what to say and what not to say, what will help and what will harm.

I collect Zach and pop his dirty laundry in the trunk of the car.

"Just one night, Zach," I explain. As much as I want to fix him with a spell in the country and a mother's unerring affection, I know that any longer than twenty-four hours might not be the best remedy for either of us. A longer stay will not only exhaust me, trying to adapt to his nocturnal clock, but also sabotage his chances of being allocated supported accommodation through a social services care package. The professionals will see his needs as being met and will not deem his housing situation a priority. This, I have discovered, is a conundrum for so many families both here and in the USA.

Back at Holly Farm, I pull out the sofabed in the living room. Zach puts the television on and wanders around like a cat exploring its new habitat. He sniffs at the food I am preparing.

"Go to the bathroom and wash your hands, Zigs," I say, "and lather them for at least twenty to thirty seconds."

"I washed them before I left," he grumbles.

I think about the three other tenants who use the main door to his block, and maybe their visitors too. Daily virus bulletins stress the importance of hand washing, how the soap breaks down the layer of fat protecting the virus, how it is the most effective measure we have until a vaccine can be developed.

"Zach," I say, my voice rising, along with my pulse and blood pressure.

He saunters into the bathroom and barely touches the soap. He probably thinks it is toxic.

With the bombardment of frightening images in the media, and the fact that so little is known about this virus, I am triggered. I am scared for him, and of him. I was scared for him once before, back in 2009 in the laundry room in Hollywood, and now I want to either run away in case he becomes contagious or lock him up to stop him from going into public places. I want to force him to wash his hands. But I can't. He isn't a little boy.

After supper he wants to get a fizzy drink, but I am ready for bed, and the nearest shop that is still open is five miles away. I try to be firm. I think about some of the mums from my NAMI group in California. Their sons or daughters live with them. Are they stricter than me? More tolerant than me? Why am I still unable to lay down the law in a fashion that Zach respects? The mothers I know who refuse to have their kids living with them have worked hard to untangle themselves from being so enmeshed. At first sight, they appear to live in freedom, although I see the wounds that they still carry just beneath their smiles. I also see how they fill their time with advocacy.

Zach is still watching television when I retire for the night. My room has two single beds pushed together, and I am grateful for the chance to sprawl out. At some point in the night, Zach creeps in and lies on top of the other single bed in his outdoor clothes. I shift my bed a few inches away, wishing the property had separate quarters. But my hunch is that even if I had rented such a perfect place, Zach would still want to be close to me. He needs company. Humans are social animals, especially when we are not feeling safe.

It is early morning, before dawn. Midge wakes me to go out. Zach follows us outside and we stare at the constellations, the dots of silver dancing in the dark sky.

Zach has had a fascination for astronomy since his second year of middle school. So many evenings, as we sat as a family at the big oak dinner table, he told us about supernovas and the big bang theory. He interviewed UCLA Professor Andrea Ghez about black holes and red dwarves. Ghez would later go on to win a Nobel Prize for her work to prove the existence of a supermassive black hole at the center of the Milky Way.

I could never really profess to understand these things any more than I could fathom Zach's love of chess and Shakespeare, but it didn't stop me asking him over and over again how it all worked, how everything moved in the great sky, and how it affected the tides. Sometimes he shook his head and said arrogantly, "You wouldn't understand," which was true. "But I want to try," I told him. "I want to try to make sense of it all."

Sometimes, when Zach feels unsafe these days, I lead him back to the stars and planets. I ask him questions about the things he still knows, the places that the psychiatric drugs and the trauma haven't invaded, where we can hide out and briefly come together, where he can still be my teacher, and I can take refuge in the magic of his lesson.

When the light comes up, Zach doesn't want to walk and see the public bridle path I discovered, nor does he fancy fish from the smokehouse. He wants to get back to Dereham and Morrisons for a meal deal of chips, a sandwich and a fizzy drink. With his clean laundry and iPhone in hand, he returns to his room without much ado.

He texts me before I leave the town center to say he needs his daily allowance. I pull over to transfer it to his account. I have been rationing his funds for years now; he has gotten used to it ever since the days when he used to mismanage them. Now it is as if he is frightened to budget for himself. I want to put this responsibility and so many others safely back in his hands.

The next day, worried by the idea that I might get Covid, and Zach will be left without support, I call to persuade him to work with his mental health team. A part of me knows that they do not see Zach as a priority. He is eating and drinking, and not trying to jump from a bridge or an overpass. He hasn't hurt anyone. The team has learned to respond only to the most risk-laden situations, while hoping that everyone else will just get through the night.

When Zach's phone keeps going to voicemail, I drive over. He has left his door open. He is in a deep sleep in a room as steamy as the Korean spa I used to frequent in Los Angeles. The shower is running at full capacity. Rivulets of brown, stained water trickle down the walls of the bedroom. The bathroom floor is soaked. I try to rouse him.

"What on earth are you doing?" I ask over the noise of the spray, before turning off the water. When he finally comes around, he nonchalantly tells me he needs the shower for white noise, to drown out the voices.

"But you're damaging the property! We'll have to pay for the repairs. You could be evicted."

I don't want to be wading in this mess anymore. I leave the room to find the hotel manager. In the past I would never have conceived of reporting Zach's behavior, but these recent years have pulled something so taut in me, I might snap. It is fear. I am driven by it. Fear and desperation.

I tell the manager what has happened, and ask if she wants to accompany me to Zach's room. I know he will deny her access once I have left. She agrees, and identifies the brown ribbons cascading down the wall as nicotine.

"The last person must have smoked in here."

Zach pulls the cover over his head and ignores us.

Outside in the parking lot, the manager says she will talk to the housing officer.

"I'm worried about him being evicted, especially now," I mutter, wondering if reporting the incident was a mistake. "Please make sure he doesn't end up on the street. He's too vulnerable."

I return to say goodbye to Zach, but he has locked his door.

"I'll come back tomorrow, Z," I shout. I think I can hear the shower running again.

I don't sleep well. I call the crisis team and ask for a welfare check. The next morning when we meet in Zach's room, the care coordinator surveys the brown stains, now dry and etched onto the walls. Zach is wrapped up like a mummy in his sheet, silent as the night.

"Untidy as it is, this is a good thing," the coordinator says. "We can see evidence that he has been eating and drinking."

My sense of despair heightens.

"What can I do?" I ask in the parking lot outside.

"Unfortunately, he may have to get worse before we can help him."

I have heard these things before. Too many times. They make no sense.

"Hospital and medicine don't help. He just needs a safe place to live with kind people who can listen to him," I reiterate, feeling like a broken record. "I am able to pay," I add.

"We can't deal with housing," she says.

Housing can't deal with housing either, it seems. The housing officer needs social services to approve supported living. But social services can't do anything if Zach is too distrustful to ask for help. On it goes: a wretched vicious cycle, the true meaning of insanity, if ever there was one.

I am on my way back to the cottage, wiping tears from my face, wondering how I can still cry over Zach more than a decade on, when I see lights flashing in my rearview mirror. Police.

"Fuck."

I pull over and put my head in my hands on the dashboard.

One of the officers comes to my window. I open it gingerly.

"We have been following you since you left the parking lot at the King's Head," he says. "You seem to be driving rather erratically. You had lots of time to pull out, but you hesitated unnecessarily, and then exited dangerously close to an oncoming vehicle."

"I'm sorry," I start. "I'm worried about my son. He isn't doing well. I don't normally drive a big vehicle like this, on this side of the road. I've been living in the USA." I draw breath.

"Have you been drinking alcohol?"

"No, not a drop."

The officer asks me to get out of the vehicle and walk in a straight line. He produces a breathalyzer and instructs me on how to puff into it. In all my years of driving I have never had to do such a thing.

"Can I remove the tube from the package myself?" I ask. "I'm worried about you touching it because of the virus."

He looks at me as if I am too emotional to argue with. When my sobriety is confirmed, he sends me on my way. I am shaken. In the USA I would probably have been fined, so I feel fortunate that I just got a warning. Maybe the world is asking me to pay attention, to sit up and take notice, to find sanity somewhere. Maybe if I do, Zach might follow suit.

LOCKDOWN

My phone is blowing up. All the news channels I subscribe to are pinging.

It isn't just London. The entire country is about to go into lockdown.

Lockdown. One word. It streams across my newsfeed.

I switch on the television. Boris Johnson addresses the nation.

"We must all stay at home to protect the NHS amid the growing threat of coronavirus. The police will have the power to fine people if they leave their homes for any reason other than the following:

Shopping for necessities.

One form of exercise a day—either alone or with members of your household.

Travel to work—but only if necessary and if you cannot work from home.

Medical need, or to provide care to a vulnerable person."

"Oh, thank god," I say, taking in the last point.

I reach Dale. California has been in lockdown for four days. He has had to stop surfing, and Brazilian Jujitsu too. Against all instincts he is forced to stay home. He already has cabin fever.

I throw Midge onto the backseat of the car, exhale and head over to Dereham. Zach has already been to the supermarket, which is promising, yet scary because he refuses to wear a mask. I try to think positively, recalling the days on end when he was completely bedbound with fear and a mood as flat as the East Anglian Fens. At least he is awake now, and partaking in the world.

"I want to have a proper talk with you," I say. I explain the lockdown regulations.

"Let me just finish this," he says, engrossed in a computer game on his phone.

I wait impatiently for him to put down the phone, which he finally does.

"Do you want to speak to your doctor to get some antipsychotic medicine, just in case? How about an inhaler for your asthma? I know you haven't had an attack for years, but it's good to be prepared."

"Not yet," Zach says, picking up his phone again.

"It's about being practical," I say. I stand a fair distance from him with my t-shirt pulled up over my nose and mouth. It is the way I used to find Zach so often in the past, and now I mimic the action, feeling the neck of the garment taut across my face.

"If we wait, it might be harder to get what we need. There could be a big demand. If I get sick, I won't be able to pick anything up for you."

"It's fine," he says. "Can we go for a drive?"

I wonder if he has really forgotten the rules so quickly, or if I am not as loud as his other voices and he never quite heard me in the first place.

"No, it isn't allowed," I say. I look around at the mounting pile of empty takeaway cartons, remnants of food and dirty washing. I don't touch anything. I have read reports that the virus can live on surfaces: on fabrics, on cardboard, on foil, on plastic, on metal.

"Are you going to clean up?" I ask.

"Yes," he answers, but makes no attempt.

"I'm taking Midge to Neatherd Moor," I say.

Zach reaches for his shoes. This will be his second outing of the day. I am grateful. But at the park entrance, I ask him not to get too close. I stay a few paces behind, watching as he moves his hands in his pockets, his frame narrower than it has been in so long. I worry my vigilance might make him feel worse, but I can't help myself. He could be asymptomatic, a carrier. He could feel sick and not tell me. He doesn't say much these days, not to me anyway, but I hear him shouting out loud in response to the voices in his head. He sometimes puts his fingers in his ears to try to block them out.

My watch says 11:11. I close my eyes. According to Carolyn, our acupuncturist back in California, we should take notice of this supposedly divine number. I always pray for the same thing when the clock strikes this time. I meditate on the same wish when I blow out my birthday candles: for Zach to live with less fear. For my youngest son to find his way, not just for a moment, or for a day, but for life.

As we are walking back to the King's Head, Gordon calls to tell me that his doctor has notified him that he is in the clinically vulnerable category.

"I can't leave the house or have any visitors for twelve weeks." He coughs, as if I don't believe him.

"How will you manage?" I ask, although he should be the one asking me.

It is ironic that we landed here so Zach could spend time with his father, yet now it is everyone for him or herself. Zach and I, through necessity, are in our own bubble. Gordon is in his.

"I hope we can still visit the place I found for Zach," I say. "I want to go home, just for a while."

"It isn't classed as essential business," Gordon reminds me.

He is right—the staff will help us set up a video call for a cyber-tour of the accommodation, but no visits and no new admissions are allowed at this time.

I try to strategize, calling Zach's care coordinator, social worker and housing officer. "I want to put a plan in place, in the event that I become unavailable," I repeat to each one of them.

It feels futile. Everyone will be working from home. Zach can call his team if he wants to talk, which I can pretty much guarantee he will not. The manager of the King's Head has been instructed to close the communal areas of the hotel. Zach is all at once more vulnerable than ever, in his room in the old stable block with no face-to-face service providers.

I want to keep him safe, but everything is grinding to a halt. Most importantly, I know that sooner or later we will receive a letter discharging him from services.

Some psych wards both here and in America have been designated as Covid-19 wards for sectioned patients who test positive. If beds were few and far between before Covid, now they are even scantier. Vulnerable folks who are sectioned often lie on a gurney for days, or stay in police custody until a bed becomes available.

The admissions officer at the home I have been counting on explains that it may be a while until they can offer Zach a place. I realize I cannot leave now, not now, maybe never. Walking away seems like the cruelest measure I could inflict upon both of us. I know I cannot save him, but at least I can be with him.

Nance is still hoping that Together UK will deliver, but I know that Zach's situation does not consume her. At times I envy her, want to be her. I want to be Gordon. I want to be Dale. I want to be anyone but me. I want to disappear, to never have to come in from the outdoors, where the flat Norfolk landscape grounds me, where I have long views, and a level perspective for miles.

Zach's neighbors tell me they sometimes see him walking in the road at night in bare feet. They insist that I need to do something. Other times he wanders off into the moorland on cold nights without a coat. I see him as a little dot on my phone screen via an app that tracks his whereabouts. I agonize over it all—his autonomy, mine, how much time I should let pass before calling the police.

Norfolk is dull on this particular day. The gray sky and sea blend effortlessly like a Steiner palette, reminding me of a particular mid-winter shift that I did at Año. I had been posted with another docent at the lookout above Cove Beach. Sheltering under our waterproof ponchos, heads down against the wind and the spray, she told me about the rogue waves of late, and how they had carried away six people so far.

"You can't ever turn your back on the ocean," she said. "You can have five or six calm waves, but that seventh one will knock you off your feet."

As we discussed the dangers of the Northern Californian coast, a man approached us. He was very well kitted out in sporty rainproof attire, an expensive pair of binoculars around his neck. I thought he would ask about the elephant seals. But he was not interested in the seals, or the birds, or the endangered San Francisco garter snake— he was looking for the body of a twelve-year-old boy who had been swept out to sea thirty miles up the coast a few days earlier.

"He was wearing a green t-shirt and a pair of white shorts," said the man, who was part of the search party.

I was struck by the tale. The boy had been dragged under along with his father and eight-year-old brother, but the sea had spat the other two out on that warm holiday afternoon. Search and rescue had called off their operation after two days, but his family wanted his body back so they could bury him. It was a way to grieve, to achieve closure, but I wondered whether the boy's father would truly be able to rest. He had turned his back on the water, and he had survived when his child hadn't.

I knew that my pain was different, and I hadn't lost a child to drowning, but I found myself unable to stop thinking about the family. I kept a look out for the green of a t-shirt, the white of a pair of shorts. Watching the news on my computer that night, I saw her, the boy's mother with her head bowed, unable to speak or look at the camera. I could not bear to witness her pain. Yet I could not let go of this tragedy. It was as if I knew this family, as if it were mine. Zach had been twelve when he had first come to this place. I thanked everything in the world that kept him here with us on earth.

In Cranworth, at the cottage, I try to ride with the current of the pandemic and not fight against it. Some days I agree to drive Zach out to the beach, keeping the car windows open, hoping we won't get stopped. Zach seems more peaceful during these trips. He gazes out of the window, silently observing the empty roads, refusing to get out at the destination, but rather asking me to keep driving. Like me, he wants to be in constant motion. He wants to revisit the past too, sharing memories, sometimes disagreeing with me and saying he is twelve thousand years old, or from Australia, or adopted, that he knows the truth. I stay silent. I have at least learned something.

On the day I call Zach's doctor, he agrees that due to extenuating circumstances he will prescribe an inhaler and antipsychotic medication without needing to speak to Zach. I ask if it is possible for me to join the doctor's office as a temporary patient. The administrative staff agree that I can be placed on the register. Temporary patients are not eligible for routine medical procedures, but I can receive life-saving measures should I contract Covid. I am overcome with relief.

I set off for Swaffham, winding along the country lane that leads to the Manor Farm Practice. Giant windmills dominate the landscape, mechanized beasts slicing the air with their metal arms. It is otherworldly—the silence, my solitary presence on the road, the thick hedges that line both sides of the single track. I miss Nance. I wish she could see this view.

I am passing Southend Lane when the radio comes on, startling me. It is Classic FM, mum's favorite radio station, the one that woke her up in the morning and lulled her to sleep at night. It has come to life as if by magic. Even more peculiar is the fact that Bruch's violin concerto is playing, the piece she loved so fiercely that we chose it for her funeral. I pull over into the deserted entrance to a farm, and I weep.

I had only tolerated classical music and opera until my brother, Dan, in a fit of generosity, paid for us three siblings and mum to go to Verona, the birthplace of her beloved Giuseppe Verdi, in her final days. "It's so different onstage," she whispered as we sat in the open-air amphitheater, in the dark, with Mars visible in the night sky. She held my hand as the quartet sang and the violins cut through the still-warm air. It brought me to tears, the sorrow I felt for the jilted lovers, for myself, for mum. I wonder if she knew it would stay with me, this legacy of being truly moved by music.

I turn up the volume and hum along, my voice crackly with emotion. I decide to tell Zach about it later.

At the doctor's office, after I fill out the new patient form, I wait in a line in the parking lot to pick up the prescriptions. The man in front turns around to talk. I pull the mask I have fashioned from my t-shirt tighter around my nose and mouth.

"We should drop a bloody bomb on those Chinese," he says. "They eat cats and dogs, you know."

I feel suffocated by his hatred, and the gagging nature of my t-shirt mask.

Mum would have said something.

"That is very rude," I say, wagging a finger, like I am telling off a child.

"Shoot the fucking lot of them," he retorts.

When I stop off at Dereham with the drugs, Zach is staring at the ceiling. This would constitute a down day, seriously down. I sit on the bed, while Midge licks his cheek.

"Shall I put on some music?" I ask. Zach nods.

I tell him what happened in the car. "I know it sounds absurd, but I feel like she came to me." He doesn't ridicule me. Maybe he is closer to the ancestral spirits in his altered state.

I place my phone between us, and the voices of Maria Callas and Pavarotti fill the humble room. I am thankful that Zach loves music. His eyes, which seem to change from gray to green to amber depending on the light or his mood, are today a soft hazel. His mouth puckers ever so slightly. I can tell he is moved.

"Are you okay, Mum?" he asks. He rarely wants to know how I am, and often does not believe I am his mum, so this is a gift.

I play "Easter Hymn," the intermezzo from *Manon Lescaut*, and of course Bruch's violin concerto. As the sound resonates, I pledge an oath: I will try not to act out of fear, to coerce or cajole. I will be more accepting, of Zach, of myself, of the lockdown. I am safe. Zach is alive. Through the gift of music, I have mum in my life again.

"I love you, Zigs," I say on my way out. "The drugs are in the bag on your shelf, a low dose. It's up to you, okay? Your choice completely. But remember that coming down slowly is easier on your brain than going cold turkey."

I think about the bargaining I have used over the years. *You can live with us if you take your drugs. You can have a little flat of your own if you take the injectable. You can go to the UK if you stick with the pills.* Zach always maintained the drugs were toxic, unnecessary, made him feel sluggish, sedated, fat. Nothing about them makes this an easy choice. Coming off them is like climbing Mount Everest, staying on them is like dying on the mountain. But I can't be the drugs police anymore. I know it was a mistake ever believing that they would be a magic cure-all.

As well as those with lived experience of this thing we call psychosis and their family members, there are many psychiatrists and psychotherapists around the world who have shared the same "oh fuck" moment as I am having now. Dr. James Davies, psychotherapist and author of *Cracked: Why Psychiatry is Doing More Harm Than Good*, has revealed that despite tens of billions of pounds being spent on psychiatric research in the last two decades, 18 billion pounds being pumped into the NHS mental health budget annually and twenty-five percent of the adult population being prescribed psychotropics each year, the outcomes for those who are treated has gone from bad to worse. Psychiatrist Joanna Moncrieff, a founding member of the Critical Psychology Network, is also skeptical of the idea that mental disorders are simply diseases of the brain. She campaigns to reduce the influence of the pharmaceutical industry and find alternatives to narrow medical-model-based practice.

These ideas are controversial, but I believe them to be worthy. Some truths are hard to live with, especially when they are up against the power of big business and the dominant paradigm. All I can do is try to trust, to give Zach more agency, to keep myself as well as I can, so I can be here for him in this world for as long as possible.

Midge and I walk at least five, six or seven miles a day, despite the rules allocating just one hour of exercise. I jog at night as the sun goes down over the common. I visit Zach each evening to drop off food. He is often asleep, but if he is awake, we watch a little television, he pets Midge, and I try hard not to worry about catching or spreading the virus.

As the lockdown separates me physically from everyone else aside from Zach, the feeling of camaraderie and the explosion of online platforms like Zoom connects me to people I haven't spoken to in eons. I converse with Nance daily, too, having FaceTime tours of the farm, seeing the new additions—two goats and a rooster that visit our cabin. Nance names the bird Cock Hudson and makes him a ladder so he can roost in a tree and not get eaten by coyotes.

I offer to buy Zach a tablet in the hope that he will be able to connect to people too, to access support that has moved online, to play chess. He isn't keen on the idea of having a new electronic device. He doesn't trust technology right now.

My screen time goes up instead of down in my search for solace in the cottage. I start Iyengar yoga classes online with our friend Lisa who now lives in France, and return to my Swaffham based teachers Mike and his wife Camilla. Instead of driving to their light-filled studio in their Georgian home, the practice is via Zoom. This couple will eventually become my dear friends as well as my teachers. All of us brought together through this uncertain, challenging time.

Twice a week I saunter into the living room at Holly Farm cottage, often still in my pajamas. I roll out my mat and put my body into positions that stretch me: downward facing dog (Adho Mukha Svanasana), child's pose (Balasana) and warrior one (Virabhadrasana).

I feel like a warrior, but that is different from being resilient. Being a warrior means pushing and fighting to the end. Being resilient comes from acceptance and growth. I want to be resilient. I want to learn to do nothing. I want to resist the desire to react to Zach's situation with force. Aside from the external change in the seasons and the landscape, Lisa talks of change within, and tells us how everything will pass.

"Change is not something we should fear," she tells us, quoting BKS Iyengar, the founding father of this style of yoga. "Rather, it is something we should welcome."

It is a timely message. In the Jewish tradition it is called Passover. In the book of Exodus, the God of Israel inflicts ten disasters on Egypt to force the Pharaoh to free the Israelites from slavery. The pandemic is a disaster, only instead of being plagued by water turning to blood, frogs, lice, flies, livestock pestilence, boils, hail, locusts, darkness and the killing of first-born children, we have a virus that attacks the lungs and spreads like wildfire. I don't relish Matzoh (unleavened bread), or the bitter herbs used for the telling of the Haggadah—the story of the Exodus—at Passover, but it is the coming together of people for the ritual feast, or Seder, and the liberation at the heart of the tale that I admire, that I seek for myself, for Zach, for us all.

LESSON

The mental health system, as broken as it was before, is barely held together by a band-aid now. I fear that the pandemic is the only thing stopping Zach from being evicted. Laws are in place to stop people from moving about. I am sure it is just a matter of time, though, before he will be asked to leave because he is unable to take care of the property.

Stepping back as much as I am doing feels like turning my back on a rogue wave in California, the kind that took that child away. I don't even know what I am waiting for anymore, other than the moment in which Zach might perhaps rise from all of this and find meaning.

Claire Bidwell Smith's book, *Anxiety: the Missing Stage of Grief*, helps me to make sense of the dysregulation of my nervous system, my fast shallow breathing, a trembling sensation triggered by thoughts of the past. Dale feels the effects of past trauma too. Normally private about his emotional state, he begins to talk over Facebook Messenger. We share strategies that involve deep breathing, shaking our limbs, and taking cold showers. Dale introduces me to Bessel van der Kolk's *The Body Keeps the Score*. I learn why I find it so hard to stay away from Zach. The fear has set alight the fight-or-flight reactions in the circuitry of my brain and dampened down the areas that support resilience. It lives in my body. It keeps me stuck. It keeps me scared. It is a real thing. Not my fault. I am like a veteran who has fought a long, bloody battle on many foreign fronts. I need to be conscious of how to breathe, to self-regulate whenever the need arises so I can be available to Zach, but not take away his agency, or allow others to do so.

I know I deserve some self-compassion, yet still there are times—plenty of them—when I envy "normal" people their "normal" activities. The smell of a barbecue on a bank holiday afternoon, the sight of a family out for a bike ride, a conversation with someone who raves about how well their son is doing, how they have a grandchild on the way, makes me feel winded. I am even jealous of my therapist, Karen in Northern California, with whom I still have the odd session when I am unsure of how to behave. She has a wife and two sweet daughters; one birthed by her, the other by her wife. She gets to stay at home with her entire family. As much as Karen—a strong lesbian role model—has helped me, which is a lot, she cannot fix me, and I cannot fix Zach, and we remind each other of this until I become too exhausted to talk and listen anymore. I see how easy it must be for Zach to shut down.

Nance tells me I am making progress. Zach seems to be happier too. We are like a hanging mobile. As I swing into a new position, so does everyone else in the family.

I catch Zach giggling to himself. He shares the fact that a bird has spoken to him, or one of his voices has said something kind or witty. He looks like he used to, as if he is having a joke with a good friend, until one night in April, when he calls me at 9:20 p.m. to tell me he has been beaten up.

I drive over to find him sitting in the corner of his room holding his jaw and wincing in pain. He has been punched in the temple, in the jaw and twice on the forehead. The swelling to the temple worries me most. His eye is already starting to mottle, turning deep purple.

"I was outside Morrisons. I didn't do anything, I just asked them to stop talking about me," he says.

"What the bloody hell? I should call the police."

"The guy knocked me to the floor. His girlfriend, I think it was his girlfriend, just watched."

"Maybe we should call the paramedics as well. Did you lose consciousness?"

"No, I don't think so." He is shaking and confused.

I feel violated that someone has done this to my son.

"If Doubles had been with me this wouldn't have happened, would it?" Zach asks. Doubles is Zach's nickname for his brother, short for Double D, a silly tag he gave him years ago. But Dale, the Jujitsu expert, was too far away to protect Zach, and so was I.

I run a piece of kitchen towel under cold water and hold it to Zach's eyelid. I also try to get through to the police, but there is no answer. The station is close by, so I leave Zach and go there. It is all locked up. A sign instructs visitors to use a yellow telephone receiver outside the front office to connect with someone. I hold the phone gingerly to my ear, wondering who may have done so beforehand, and if it might make me sick. The phone rings and rings and rings but there is no answer. I return to Zach, vowing to call later.

"We need to catch these bastards," I tell Zach.

I want to take photographs of his grotesquely bashed face for evidence, but Zach refuses, hiding under the quilt.

"Can you get me some ice from somewhere?" he asks.

I drive to the garage, as everywhere else is closed. There is no ice. There are no popsicles, no frozen peas, nothing to help reduce the swelling. The hotel, of course, is shut. I hate this fucking pandemic.

"I thought you said I would be safe here?" Zach says to me when I return.

Somewhere in the region of my heart, my thorax and deep in my throat, I hurt so profoundly I need to sit down.

The paramedics come out, but Zach refuses to go to the hospital to get an x-ray. Part of me is relieved. It feels just as dangerous to get in an ambulance and go to the emergency room as it does to live in a town where people ignore the sight of someone being beaten up outside a supermarket. It crushes me, as do Dale's words when I get through to him later that night. "I wish I had been there," he says. "If only I had fucking well been there."

The attack puts Zach back in a place I haven't witnessed him in for many years. He stays in bed, too scared to go out. He stops calling me and answering his phone.

I speak to the police and to the staff at Morrisons. There were no witnesses. The cameras can only be examined if Zach gives his permission and provides ID. He will not. I ask him if he wants to stay at the cottage with me. He does not. He stops speaking.

I believe that the attack will show the team that Zach really needs more oversight and protection than I can provide, which it does, but I still meet a wall. Zach's social worker does not believe that he qualifies for supported living. I cannot convince her otherwise.

I turn to the assessment manager at Together UK. She is concerned that Zach is nocturnal and may not be suitable for her accommodation. It costs more to have someone awake on night duty. A staff member sleeps at the facility, but she should not be disturbed unless there is an emergency.

I want to reset Zach's body clock so he can become diurnal again, yet I know that he has to do more than just wake up in the morning. He needs to be able to trust again, to forgive those who have taken so much away from him, to find his people. He needs to feel safe enough to want this for himself, not for me.

I am beginning to recognize that I have been begging for help that is not helpful, that has never come without strings attached. I can't make Zach move into one of the residential homes any more than I can force him to take the drugs. Or cure him. Although I gave him a body, he has his own spirit. This is the greatest lesson I must learn.

•

On one of my last shifts at the elephant-seal colony, I was asked to stand sentry on New Year's Creek Beach where an injured elephant seal had hauled out. It was harder to access than the other viewing areas, necessitating a scramble across a couple of boulders to get around the creek and onto the sand.

The waves were forceful, with surf spraying high into the air. The reserve wanted to make its final mark on me, it seemed. I took my seat on a huge washed-up log on the beach. Up close, the water looked like it could have breached the shoreline and pulled me out and under. It didn't. The waves broke thirty feet away, but that didn't stop me from fearing them.

Mavericks, home to some of the largest swells in the world, was not that far north of here, and the Farallon islands, twenty-seven miles offshore from San Francisco, had the highest numbers of white sharks in the region.

I pulled my red docent cap down, fighting the wind. Año Nuevo was shrouded by a bank of marine fog, making me feel quite cut off. My charge, an adolescent male elephant seal, made me balk. He was huge. Based upon his size alone, and the length of his nose, I judged him to be around seven or eight years old, a sub-adult. Through my binoculars I saw the scar on his back. It looked like a cookie cutter shark bite.

I approached him carefully, noticing how exhausted he seemed, propped onto one side of his massive body, oblivious to the water that was lashing just feet away. He stayed very still. I wondered if he was in pain. It was my job to safeguard this stray isolated juvenile bull, the same way it had been my duty to sit with Zach in the early days, then weeks and finally months. Sometimes Zach wanted me to perch on his bed so he could get to sleep, other times he asked me to just be there during his waking hours.

"I'm scared about how it will end," was his common refrain. "Please tell me if you know."

"It won't end badly. You will live for a long time, a good life, doing things that fulfill you," I used to tell him. But it scared me too, this uncertainty.

The seal flipped his tail in the sand like a rudder. I checked again to make sure he was a male, because females do this movement when they are about to give birth. I couldn't see his sex organs from where I sat, but with the laws of nature as they are, this big guy with his huge head and long nose was not going to be bearing a calf.

After a few minutes, a hiker with a walking stick fashioned from eucalyptus came wading through the creek in wellington boots. He asked me about the beach and the rock formation, then saw the seal and asked to take a picture. I allowed him to get twenty-five feet away and snap the shutter.

The seal lumbered backward, his blubber shifting and quivering.

Another three hikers crossed the creek and came onto the beach. A young woman screeched in excitement as she spotted the seal. I saw him twitch his long nose. I wanted to tell her to be quiet. This was this majestic animal's habitat, and she was in the seal's bedroom. She was being invasive.

But I didn't. I just glared and tightened my grip on my walkie-talkie radio, making sure the channel was set to number two. The woman and the rest of her group gave the seal a wide berth and disappeared around the cliffs.

I returned to the log until my butt grew numb. The wind lessened. I watched the sun dip, making a wide silver strip on the water. The seal seemed to be enjoying it, taking in the warmth, the rhythmic boom of the waves, the shifting of sand and pebbles on the shore.

I knew from my training that he was better at hearing sounds underwater than in the air, partly due to the middle ear adapting to the pressures found at the depths to which he dived. It had always intrigued me to know that animals hear sounds at different frequencies from humans—and some humans, many more than is commonly understood, hear voices, or sounds that nobody else is able to hear.

My contemplation was cut short by a couple rounding the creek with a pit bull terrier. I approached them, radio in hand, and explained that the injured elephant seal was close by. They offered to retreat, and I thanked them. I went back to staring at the seal, hoping he would recuperate and join the rest of the seals up at North Point.

When it was just the two of us—me and the seal—I moved closer than I probably should have. I snapped a photo of the wound and enlarged it on my phone. It was deep and pink, with yellow in the center, as if something had chewed right down into the blubber.

"Please be okay, fella," I said, competing with the sound of the waves.

The injured seal raised his head, and his tail then flopped down onto the sand. He did it again and again. As I was about to leave, he lifted his head and vocalized, the sounds muffled by the wind and the spray. His unique signature call got louder as he slithered toward the water.

Was he strong enough, well enough, to be in the water? I didn't want the wound to attract predators. I saw his dark shape as he moved north toward the harem on the next beach. I contemplated hiking up to the North Point to see if I could spot him, but the sun was sinking lower, and Highway 1 would grow dark soon. I needed to hustle.

I sensed that I might not see this seal again, not unless I returned to America at exactly the right time and noticed his telltale battle scar when he hauled out onto North Point to molt, or to High Willow to mate. He would have to continue to face danger in the water, whether I saw him again or not, and I knew that being with him today was the best I could do. It was the best he could do, too, this wounded warrior beast.

2 0

HOME

When a mother orca or dolphin gives birth, the other females in the pod are heavily invested in the offspring. They help the calf to the surface to take its first breath. If the calf dies the pod doesn't let go, but gathers around and stays with the new mother for some time, supporting her in her journey. This can go on for days, this shared tour of grief. At some point the pod will stop pushing the calf to the surface, but it will still hunt for food for the cetacean mother. It will not abandon her.

In Norfolk, I find my own pod. It is called Safely Held Spaces. There are five of us, all mothers of those who have experienced psychosis. Every Wednesday at 7 p.m. we meet online. We laugh. A lot. Sometimes we cry, me especially. When we surface from the pain, we understand what it means to hold each other, to not turn away.

We agree that we are all mad, all disordered, all traumatized, and our loved ones are no different from anyone else. More sensitive, more empathic perhaps, but they are just fighting this battle on the front lines.

Zach starts to rally again, slowly, trusting that he can talk to me, and leave the bed and breakfast to walk with me and Midge. He wonders if we can still go to Spain together to walk the Camino de Santiago, and to Costa Rica as a family, like we often talked about, so that he and Dale can surf. He wants to get a part-time job that isn't too taxing, have a dog of his own, play guitar in a band.

When he asks, "Where is the best place for me?" we discuss a therapeutic farm community in Scotland, and Soteria houses. These are homes, not hospitals: affordable, peer-run and with no forced medication. Healing takes place through relationships. Zach is curious. The decision will be up to him.

At night, to help me sleep, I log onto the Año Nuevo livestream, a camera that is set up to record the views and sounds of the island, twenty-four hours a day. Even with my eyes closed, I recognize the barks of the California sea lions, the noisiest of animals, and the deep, rumbling belching sounds of the elephant seals.

If I wake up in the early hours, anxious about Zach being alone, I breathe. Eight seconds in through the nose. Eight seconds out. The Wi-Fi is strongest just before dawn, and sometimes the livestream reconnects on its own. I hear the wind, the waves. They lull me back to sleep like a hammock aboard a ship.

When the morning sun comes up, I open the kitchen windows to the sound of the birds. There are many different species that make the East Anglian marshland their home.

Home. I miss having my own home. I miss Nance. She is getting ready to sell our old house in Hollywood—the one where Zach first set us on an unexpected path from the laundry room—so we can look for a place together here in England. I need to hold on to this. My hope is that Zach will visit us at weekends and holidays. Dale has decided that he likes to be in the UK too. After so long, we might finally all be together again on the same continent.

My friend Debs loves the idea of us moving up near her and sends me listings for places up on the Lancashire moors. "We want an old fixer upper," I say. "If I can't fix Zach, then I want to at least fix something."

•

It is the beginning of August 2020 when I hit upon the idea. There is a seal colony at Blakeney Point in Norfolk. A boat goes out from Morston Quay and circles the sandbank where the country's largest display of common and gray seals lives. These are my elephant seals' English cousins. I want to go and see them.

The lockdown halted these seal tours like it did so much else, but restrictions are gradually easing. Nobody had been out there until two weeks ago, when the government reopened the National Trust parking lots and gave the boat tour operators the authority to take people out again.

Passengers must wear masks and occupancy has been reduced from twenty-five to twelve people. Tickets are selling out quickly, so I have reserved ahead of time. Midge is allowed to come with me. I ask Zach if he would like to join me. He declines. I don't push. Everyone has a right to say no—especially Zach, who has not been listened to when he has said no so many times before.

A heatwave takes hold of the UK. Temperatures rise to ninety-seven degrees, but are down to seventy-two on the morning that I set off. It is still humid. I blow the cool air from the fan on the dash and hope it reaches Midge on the back seat.

Just a few miles in, there is a thunderstorm. Lightning strikes. The day turns more comfortable in minutes. The rain pours. Seals love the rain. They are more active in showers and storms. I am content. I am happy. I soak in everything. The flat, red-brick façades of the old converted barns that line the country lanes. The fields that stretch out in a subtle meander. I can tell I am getting close to the sea.

I am early for a change, so I stop off at a farm stall just three miles south of Holt to buy homemade blackberry jam and a bag of freshly picked new potatoes. I sort out three pound coins and pop them in the honesty box. I love this system. I imagine Nance joining me here. We could do the same thing, have a little table outside the front door of our farmhouse, and sell extra eggs or chutney, or whatever we can spare.

I pick up my ticket at Blakeney Point, then drive a couple of miles farther to get the boat from Morston Quay. I want to talk about seals with the tour company owner, Paul Bishop, but he is much too busy. He does tell me that the RSPCA at East Winch runs a seal sanctuary that saves sick creatures, fixes them up and returns them to the estuary. Did he say fix them up, save them, return them to the estuary? He did. He did indeed.

I think about my wild and far-away Año Nuevo. I know the difference between the two preserves is not entirely cut and dry. Ano Nuevo is a "Natural preserve" under a California state park designation. That is why animals are not saved if dying of normal life cycle causes. It is the law. In the UK, a tiny territory in comparison, with a more modest population of seals—seals that are small enough to be easily transported—preservation and intervention are more accessible.

There are other variables. The terrain is gentler here, that's for sure. The North Sea can be rough, but it isn't the Pacific. There are no sharks here, no predators to endanger the seals other than humans with their fishing nets and frisbee rings.

Here in little England, the downpour I have just driven through was a simple summer storm. Torrents of rain and booming claps of thunder, but no tectonic plate movement, no forest fires or tsunamis. It is a calm, cool day with people lining up politely for boat tickets, for ice creams, for tea and sausage rolls.

Once we are all seated, masked and socially distanced, we set sail. The boat feels timeless, an old wooden clinker with an outboard motor that chugs like a motorbike. I place Midge on my lap as the boat edges out of Morston Quays. We thread through a multitude of little moored sailboats with names like *Juno, Nimbus, Puffin, Sky, Hercules, Jackie, Jane* and *Angela*. Once we get beyond this charming cluster of vessels, the tide gets choppy. I can see where the mouth of the estuary leads into the North Sea. I tighten my grip on Midge.

The skipper tells us that by tonight there will be no water here at all. Once the tide goes out, it exposes this stretch and leaves nothing but a bed of sand and shingle. I can see the shale and the bottom of the shallow estuary when I peer over the side of the boat. Everything changes constantly here. The dunes and sandbanks are clawed away a yard at a time each year, moving the point farther and farther out.

As we gain momentum, I feel a swell of excitement in my belly, and smile in anticipation. I will probably see pups, as August is the end of the birthing season for the common seals. I will see gray seals too, and I can't bloody wait.

The skipper points the bow of the clinker toward Blakeney Point. The sandbank ahead of us is white, and the smell reminds me of Año—salty sea air and guano. The sky is dotted with sandwich and common terns who are deafeningly shrill. They are due to migrate back to the shores of Africa any day now.

On the little raised stretch of shingle, I see the animals lining the shore. The clinker draws level with them and cuts the engine. The common seals' coats are mottled brown. The gray seal pups' fur, which would have been as white as cotton just three weeks ago, is now dusky in tone. They have tripled in size, too, after feeding on their mother's rich milk. Like elephant seals, they take to the water alone.

Other similarities remind me of my beloved animals at Año Nuevo. The fact that the mothers give birth high up on the beaches in the protected dunes, and that they abandon their pups, letting them fend for themselves once they are weaned. The way they mate again, then return to the ocean, famished from feeding their young. Today I watch them scratch at the molting skin on their itchy bellies, frolicking in the water and fighting each other for dominance. It is such a tonic, this cool day on the coast.

Not everything is the same here. Two things are different, vastly so. It is safer and it is kinder. Most soothing are the statistics. More than 2,700 seals live in this rookery, a record number this year, and the mortality rate is just 2.5 percent.

As the boat skirts the point for the last time before making a wide turn to sail back to the quays, I take a final look. The seals will spend most of the year foraging for shellfish and sand-eels, of which there is a good supply in this part of the world. They don't have to venture much farther than the middle of the North Sea. They don't dive beyond seventy meters on average, and they don't stay down for much longer than five to ten minutes at a time.

I focus my binoculars on a youngster—a gray, all alone. The other pups are frolicking in the water, preparing for their first voyage. Their mothers have already left. I zoom in on his flipper. He is tagged so the sanctuary can track him, keep an eye on his feeding and dive patterns. His gaze is fixed on the horizon; he is ignoring the splashing and honking of the other pups. It is as if he is reluctant to brace the cold, open waters, wanting to make sure it is especially calm. His journey won't be perilous like that of the elephant seal pups, but I still want to cheer him on, rally him in this virgin solo voyage.

"Good luck, fella," I call out. The rest of the passengers look at me. Somehow, in this moment, I feel confident that I will revisit the sanctuary. I am not sure when, but soon.

In the interim I let go of any worry. Like so many of the gray seals, this one will return to Blakeney Point, to the same breeding site. He may have to search out higher ground because of erosion, or haul out farther along the coast at Winterton-on-Sea, but he will be back, bigger and stronger, having followed his instincts. He will know how to fish, how to dive, and how to survive in this place he has come to call home.

ACKNOWLEDGMENTS

Zig-Zag Boy is a collaboration. I am humbly grateful to everyone who gave me a helping hand. Thank you to the *New York Times*, for publishing my essay "Unmoored by a Psychotic Break" and allowing me to realize that I had a book in me. Professors Maggie Humm and Mike Davis, who insisted I could dare to write about personal things. My mentor, Cathy Madison, who shared her expertise and rooted for me as if I were family, because in some way I am.

Fellow writers Camilla Balshaw, Courtney Lund O'Neil, Sylvia Sukop and Bonnie Kaplan, who read drafts and offered love and sensitive critique. Emma Finn, my brilliant "hands-on" agent at C&W, who was smart and tenacious every step of the way. Jill Bialosky, my editor, and Drew Weitman, her assistant, at W. W. Norton, who so deftly shepherded the work from beginning to end. James Scurry and Joanna Monaghan, cofounders of Safely Held Spaces, who advised on mental health language. Año Nuevo State Park, and my mentor for the docent program, Kelly O'Connor, who patiently shared everything she knew about pinnipeds. My best friend, Janey, who just gets me as I am. The collective mothers of support groups, past and present, who know my heart so well. My Yiddisher mama who instilled in me the power of story. Auntie Betty, who gave me first an emotional space and then a physical one to be a writer. Family on both continents for embracing me—always. And of course my wife, Nance, who always believed that one day I would be able to share my writing with the world, and supported me in a myriad of ways to make sure I never gave up. My sons, Dale, of whom I am so proud because he loves his brother so fiercely and makes us all laugh, and Zach, whose indomitable spirit is still teaching me so much about myself and the world.